Come to the Light of Love

The Loving Light Books Series

Also by Liane Rich

Loving Light

Book 19

Come to the Light of Love

Liane Rich

Loving Light Books
Original Copyright © 1997
Copyright © 2012 Liane

ISBN 13: 978-1-878480-19-4
ISBN 10: 1-878480-19-7

Loving Light Books:
www.lovinglightbooks.com

Also Available at:
Amazon: www.amazon.com
Barnes & Noble: www.barnesandnoble.com

for Katie

The information in this series is not necessarily meant to be taken literally. It is meant to *shift* your consciousness....

Foreword

Anyone immersed in the vast body of new metaphysical knowledge is aware of the virtual symphony of voices from channeled sources throughout the world – inspirational voices that may be artistic, poetic, philosophical, religious, or scientific. And now, out of these myriad New Age voices, comes a series of books by God, channeled through Liane, revealing the frank truth in all its glory and wonder, telling us how to cleanse our bodies, gain access to our subconscious minds, clear our other selves and march back to who we are – God.

In God's books you will be introduced to a loving, powerful, gripping, exciting, and often humorous voice that reaches out and speaks ever so personally to the individual reader. As the reader's interest deepens, invariably an intimate relationship to this voice develops. It is a relationship that lasts forever, and I am quite certain I do mean forever.

Here is an accelerated program, a no-holds-barred course, where God guides us and loves us, and as needs be recommends books to us and even a movie or musical piece along the way. He (She) enters our lives and sees through our eyes, seeming to enjoy the ride as He guides us back to US, back to ALL. Here is a voice that is playful and informative, that is humorous and serious, that is gentle and powerfully divine. It is a voice that knows no barriers or restrictions, a straightforward and honest voice that caresses us when we need the warmth and pushes us when we are immobilized.

In today's New Age literature there is an avalanche of information from magnificent beings of light, information that possesses us and compels us to look at our fears and express our love. In this series of books by God, you will find truly powerful methods for making this transition from toxicity to purity, from density to light, from fear to love, and from the delusion of death to the awakening to full life. You will experience in these books the love and the power of God for it is your love to express and your power to behold. Rarely will you see more lucid steps for transformation. Read these beautiful words and rejoice in our period of awakening, our return to Home.

John Farrell, PhD., LCSW. – Psychologist, Clinical Social Worker, Senior Clinician Psychiatric Emergency Services, U.C. Davis Medical Center, Sacramento. John is also a retired Professor – California State University, Sacramento, in Health Sciences and Psychology.

Come to the Light of Love

Introduction

As you become accustomed to your own greatness, you will no longer find it necessary to kill off parts of you. You are the God on high that everyone praises and you are very, very intelligent. Once all parts of you are connected and reconnected, you will begin to see how you have always been the great Creator.

You are in a phase of your own self-discovery that is very difficult for many of you. You are learning to find your way around in you. You are discovering your own true identity, and you are researching your own ability to create. You are basically discovering God. You are reaching into you and you are learning to know who you are, and by doing so you are accepting more and more of you. You are so expansive that you may determine that you are too big to explore completely. However, once you have touched upon certain aspects within your creative field, you will know that you are going to be known and accepted, simply by the awareness that you create it all.

Once you learn to let go of your need to block off parts of you, you will find that you automatically improve your relationship with the creating force that lies within you. You are learning to balance all parts of you so that you no longer block the creative flow. You are unblocking you by allowing you to trust this creative flow. This, of course, is a big part of God the creator. As you remove your blocks to God the creator you will be opening up to God the creator. As you open up to God the creator, you begin to work with or alongside of this creator. You and your creator become one! You become whole. You become "love." You become a "light." You become all that is. You will then know peace and harmony. You will then know understanding and benevolence. You will then be at peace. Once you are at peace you will no longer suffer!

You will be so appreciative that you created the time and space in your life to investigate your inner realms. Space within is even more intriguing than outer-space. Inner-space is very much a part of your explorative nature and inner-space deserves your *attention*. You will find that as you explore your need to be part of the inner-space, you will be allowing yourself the opportunity to go within on a very deep level. As you learn to be a part of the connective tissue of creation, you will be associating with all that you currently are. You are no longer going to see yourself as small and insignificant. You are going to see yourself for the powerful force that you truly are. This will take some time and acceptance on your part and it will also take love. The more you love you, the greater your ability to explore and accept greater amounts of your inner workings.

You are shaping you as you go. You are becoming all that you never knew you were. You are a powerful creative force and you never even knew it until now. No one thought to tell you how you are God and you do co-create right along with God. You are two peas in a pod. It's time to come out of denial and face your very big and out-of-control fear that you may actually be the *one who creates it all*. You may actually have been around since time began. You may actually do this over and over again, and you may actually become *aware* of it for the very first time in the history of time. You will find that you have had opportunities to see yourself before, but never to this degree. The time is right. The season is here. You use seasons to grow crops and you know how to judge a good season from a bad one, and you know how to start planting at the right time so your harvest will be full and abundant.

Well, the season of awakening is upon you. This is the perfect time to wake up and know the truth. The world is waking up and humanity is waking right along with her. Humanity is affected by nature and her cycles. You are part of nature. The natural part of you is stirring and waking up now. It is a good time to wake up, and you have and will continue to prepare yourself to meet yourself. You are coming face-to-face with God only to learn that God is, and has always been, right inside of you.

As you learn to determine your own behavioral patterns, you will find that you not only belong within your own self you actually are your patterns. You are described by your personality traits and your patterns make up your traits. As you allow yourself to see how this is, you will be allowing yourself to see your own personality. You will know how you react and you will know how you behave. You will find that your behavior is directly connected to the role you are playing. If you play a victim you will find yourself suffering, as most victims suffer. If you are playing the perpetrator or bully, you will find yourself feeling tough or strong. You will also see how you hide and how you aggressively cross boundaries based on your personality type. Now that you are the biggest and the best part of yourself you will begin to see how you let go of some of these traits, and begin to allow others to be who they are without projecting one of your roles or traits onto them.

You are beginning to enter your own self and this will cause some disturbance with your old traits and patterns. Your body holds energy and you are the energy it holds. Your traits and your personality are actually held within your body. So; if body is changing and releasing old energy, it will be felt in the body. Body-aches and body-soreness could be experienced, as big chunks of old programming, or energy, begin to break loose or free themselves. This is like taking off part of you and disposing of it. It is similar to an invisible surgery. Do not be upset if you are experiencing body pain and muscle soreness for no apparent reason. You are moving into you and this forces a false you to move over in order to make room for you (the light that is you). This stretches you so you actually grow in size. This, of course, is on an energy level. You are growing into greater vibrancy, and this causes many disturbances within the old framework, or structure, of who you once believed yourself to be.

As you learn to grow and to expand, you begin to realize how you have always been here, and you have always changed and grown with the seasons. You are similar to that big old oak tree in the backyard. You do not do overnight changes, but you do constantly grow until one day you are so grand that no one wants to cut you down, and everyone wants to come look at you and marvel at the glorious beauty of it all! You are growing, expanding, shifting, increasing and vibrating at a whole new frequency. Don't you think it might cause a few physical disturbances as you go along? You are about to come into balance in certain areas of you, and these areas have been out of balance or off-center since you were a child, and some of you have carried in (or brought in) past-life stuff that made you unbalanced from birth.

You are getting tweaked and moved and fixed. Don't fight it and don't fear it. You are growing and moving and it is very good. You are learning how to be a winner in a very big way. You will be so proud and so very happy with you for making this *shift,* or move, into the light.

⚜

*A*s you begin to learn how to access all information that is stored in you, you will begin to see how you are programmed and how you can be reprogrammed and learn new ways, new habits, new ideas, new thoughts, new beliefs and above all else a new sense of direction. Once you learn to grow within your natural self you will begin to use your natural instincts, and your behavior will no longer be one of acting-out and reacting. You will begin to see how you are no longer tied to an old set of rules that inhibits you from growing beyond your current level of intelligence.

As you continue to receive intuitional as well as instinctual information, you will understand others and their needs as well as your own needs. Right now you just push to get what you want, and some of you have devised very crafty ways in which you operate. You maneuver those you can by tactics developed along your growth. You are deceitful with both yourself and with those you are seeking approval and attention from. You use your ability to control through various ways of manipulating energy to serve you best. You are not doing this because you are bad.

You taught yourself to be deceitful because you thought it would help you get whatever it was that you wanted. Many of you learned as a child how to get what you wanted from those around you. Some of you actually stumbled on ways in which you could direct your energy and get your way.

As a child, you are so intent on getting your own way that you begin to direct a great deal of attention towards such a goal. As you learn to allow your desire to shift from getting your own way to receiving from God, you will begin to drop your ways of controlling and trying to force the energy in the direction you think you want it to go. As you learn to live in the flow you will no longer be fighting against the flow, and you will no longer run-down and wear-out at such an early age. You will begin to transform and you will begin to see results.

Most of you do not realize that you manipulate and control energy in order to get what you want. A simple example of this would be to show you how you buy a gift for someone in order to show them how much you like them. You use your power with money often, and it is usually to influence others in order to get your own needs met. Not always, but a great deal of time is given to controlling how others will perceive you, and how you can impress the ones you feel are important in your life. This is control of energy. This is directing energy instead of letting things happen.

You all have experienced real giving. You just give something without really having any attachment to the outcome. When you flow, this type of giving occurs without a great deal of thought or intent. It is natural. Then we have the 'intent to please' giving, and the 'intent to regain favor' giving, and the big one which I call the 'guilt reliever' giving. These are all ways in which you choose to change the energy and redirect it. It often works for the short term but not always for the long term. This is not wrong; it is only a misguided effort to change how someone else feels about you.

Now we are going to use the flow. This way you will not end up in the wrong place, or a place that is not really conducive to your spirit. Did you ever wonder why you feel out of place in certain situations? Maybe you do not belong in a situation and would fit better elsewhere. You, of course, do not really like change, so you will fight to hold on to and to fix your current situation. You will try to bend and work the energy to what you believe "should be," instead of allowing the energy to be what it is. You will go into denial in order to stay. You do not want to give up what you have because you honestly believe that there is nothing better for you. You are not seeing how good you are and how God you are. You have lost your ability to see you through the eyes of love. You do not know how wonderful you are, and you do not see your bright and beautiful future as I do.

You will begin to realize your full potential once you have seen your own ways being created. Your ways are usually produced by your will. You "will" things into being and you "will" yourself in or out of being. Will power and its use is very poor. You will find that you are no longer concerned with will power once you learn how to flow with creation. In the past you have pushed yourself in certain directions. You never really knew if it was what you really wanted, you just thought you should go in that particular direction. You make things work for you because you do not trust that God is in charge in your life, and so you create what you "think" will bring you happiness, peace and love. It has not worked! You are not being fair with you when you push you into certain areas that stifle you. You are not being honest and you are not flowing with life force. As you learn to adjust your habits and your 'need to get pushy with energy,' you will begin to see how, in time, everything will work out very well. You are not patient so you take a million detours, when you could just sit and wait and receive what is being guided to you.

Once you adapt to this new way of dealing with energy, you will relax and trust the process. You will no longer feel so pressured to "go out and get what you want and get it now." You will calm down and you will know that you receive all that you are meant to, and you will not fall apart from being patient. You have gotten so time-pressured that you cannot enjoy peace. If you truly wish for peace of mind with no struggle, you must be willing to give up the struggle to "get enough" or "your share." You must allow the flow of creation back "in" you. You must not push it aside in order to adjust everything to your own desired speed. You have speeded your own life up and you have put pressure on you by doing this.

As you learn to go with the flow, you will discover wonderful gifts and peace of mind that will give you great pleasure. Do not be afraid to be at ease and to not be productive. I know you are pushed in business to be productive and to perform, but that is only a reflection of what you do to yourself in your personal life. As you let go of the need to perform in a specific manner to get what you desire, you will begin to question what you are desiring. Is it really that desirable, or are you acting out some long ago programmed message? Do you really want what you think you want? Are you really that determined to get it, and if you are, where did that determination originate? Was it once a big, blown-out-of-proportion fear of not having something or someone? Did you transfer your big, blown-out-of-proportion fear onto what you now so strongly think you need?

You do not need people and you do not need things. The programming is so strongly saying that you do, but it is a lie based in fear. You do not need anything, because you have the ability and the capability to draw anything that is necessary without a struggle. It is like saying you need air when air is all around you. You do not need air, you only need to open your lungs to receive what has always been right here and available.

Once you open to receive, you will open you to receive everything that has always been right here waiting for you to wake up and receive it. In the beginning, I first told Liane that she spent all of her time reaching for the big brass ring, when all the while I was standing right next to her trying to hand her the gold ring. You all do this. You ignore what is in the flow and you reach for what you desire because someone (actually many 'someones') taught you that it is what you should go after.

Sometimes the one who strongly programmed you is you. You tried to figure out how to get your way, or how to no longer get used and abused. In doing so you created a set of beliefs for yourself. Those of you, who believe you were abandoned emotionally as a child, have probably been pushing yourselves into a corner all your life. If you very ambitiously went about changing your circumstances, you will be filled with ideas about what is good and what is bad. Most often you are twisting things into two categories. It's either good for you or it's bad for you. Even if you found peace in a day, you would not see it or feel it. You would simply look for a way to fill this void or dead space. You cannot see wasting time, so you set rules and then you rule over yourself. You make sure that you get where you are going no matter what. You are determined and you are sure that this determination is a good thing.

You are pushing and driving you. You have pushed and driven certain parts of you right out of you. Do you feel driven to be better and do better? Do you feel pushed at to be better? Guess who is pushing you and guess who is driving you harder? It is you. It is all you. Depressing isn't it? You have led you into a life that is consumed with stress and pressure to be better. Here is the good news... as you allow these parts of you to return, you will be allowing the parts who "trust" to return. The parts that are most pushed out of you are those you most request. They are peace, happiness, patience, love, joy. You will receive them by asking them to return. Do not ask for a new lover or an old lover's return. Do not ask for a million dollars or a new house. Do not ask for a new job or a new car. Believe me when I say that what you most need is you! You do not need someone else or something else. You need you back!

✦

When you become full of your own essence you will begin to feel fluid in your life. You are not fluid at this point because you damned you and built barriers to stop your flow. You will find that once you let go of your own blocks, you will be able to receive yourself back into all parts of you. Once you are received back into you, you will find that you begin to receive your good. Good comes from seeing good. If you have blocks to seeing good, how can you be receiving good. You cannot receive what you do not recognize.

So; now that you have begun to rise above your unawareness, and move into information that will set parts of you free, you must begin to change. You know how much you hate to change but change is actually very good for you. Once you learn to accept change and move into a new area, you expect change to end, so you might nest and settle in. This is not change. This is simply taking one step and then stopping. I want you to take one step and then another step and then another. You are meant to flow and move. You are not meant to get stuck, both in your ways and in your ideas. You are meant to evolve and grow and change. If you are organic how can you stop growing and evolving? You cannot. You simply continue on until you are so tall that you are out of sight.

As this process of shifting and changing continues, you will find yourself being put to the test by your own rules. How can you change if you are meant to be one way, or rigid in your rules? Your rules are not flexible nor do they move. Your rules are putting you in a very big, dark hole. Your rules have criticized your every move and your rules have kept you blocked. Your rules say you are good only if you perform in such and such a manner. Your rules do not allow for deviation. You enforce and inflict your rules on yourself and on your mate and on your friends.

You also inflict and enforce your rules on your children. Your parents inflicted theirs on you, and their parents inflicted theirs on them. You also got a good dose from their parents if you had contact with them. Grandparents are very good at keeping moral issues alive and well. They love to feel as though they have all the right answers and they wish to save their children's children. To them it feels like a second chance to restore themselves and save themselves. They feel confused about their relationship with their own children, and it is easier to be less attached to the results when it comes to grandchildren.

After all, the grandchildren did not come directly from them. They were born of their offspring. This makes it less like ownership, or less like dealing with a fragment of the self.

So, as you learn to change, and to let go of your rules, you will begin to set parts of you free. These parts have been held prisoner inside of you for a very long time. Once they are set free, you will fall into balance and your life will change. You will begin to see how you do not allow yourself to be free in certain areas out of a fear that you will be punished, or hurt, or abandoned, or rejected. You will no longer create these illusions for yourself. You cannot feel rejected if you love and accept you. You cannot feel abandoned if you are "in" you. Keeping you "in" you is the greatest gift you will ever give to you. After all, you are God! If you no longer push parts of you out, you no longer push God out.

You will take on light instead of pushing away light. You will become a torch, and you will know that you are the light of your world. Your entire world will change, and you will be at peace and in love on a constant, daily basis. You will no longer be fear-driven; you will be love-driven. When love comes into you, you will no longer push love away. Love is the light that is you, that forms God.

Once you begin to heal the split within your own self, you will feel whole and complete. You will feel as though you finally calmed down and you will feel peace. This feeling of peace will assist you in healing all areas of your life and your psyche. You will be in a good mood no matter what is going on around you, because you will no longer feel turmoil within you. Your struggle will end, and you will have the information which will allow you to stay in harmony and to leave fear and fighting outside of you. You will have put you on a very nice, long vacation from struggle. No more confusion, or tension, or stress, or anger, your feelings will soften and you will flow with life.

As you learn to live in peace, you will begin to wonder at how you created so much tension in your life. Conflict is always based in fear and attached to pain. You have all experienced inner as well as outer conflict. You have all experienced fear and pain. You are now on your way to healing inner conflict, and this will make you feel much calmer and a little alone at first. You are accustomed to constant conflict within you and, as it leaves, you will or may actually feel conflicted. Once conflict is gone you may feel that you are missing something. Once big parts of you leave, you begin to feel the loss almost as you would the loss of a friend. You may feel like you have nothing or no one to call your own. You may feel at loose ends and sense a need to search for something.

The part of you that is leaving is a very big part. The loss of conflict will cause a big hole that must be filled in. This hole will gradually fill with peace. Peace takes time and will not rush at you. Peace is a very light energy and peace will make you calm. You may misinterpret this calmness as having too much free time on your hands, or as having nothing important to do in life. You will lose your edge and your edge is what has always driven you.

You will find that, as you learn to accept peace and calm, you will no longer require so much stimulation to keep you "active." You will continue to be active without feeling pushed and pressured. You will continue to live without the drudgery of dragging parts of you around with you. These parts are not so much dead in you as they are trapped in you. These parts will begin to carry their own weight. Once you learn how to be "in" you and how to "love" you, you will find it unnecessary to struggle to get ahead, because all parts of you will be working "for" you and none will be working against you. You will find ease and you will find graceful living. Your life will flow and you will be in harmony.

You are now learning to flow by allowing all trapped parts of you to come forward. They need not be pushed deep into you in an effort to get them out of you. Once you bring them out into the open, you will be free of the burdens you carry. Judgment will become a thing of the past, and guilt will gradually fade away just as bright, strong colors fade on a beach towel that is left forever in the bright sunlight. You are allowing big parts of you to fade out of existence in order to lighten and brighten your life.

As you allow these parts to fade away, you will begin to miss their presence and you may feel that something is missing in your life. It will be. Struggle will be missing, and the constant fight within your own self will be gone. You will be free and unattached. You will feel a little lonely after such a long union with such a big part of you. You will also feel sorrow. It is the sorrow of loss. The one thing you will not feel is struggle and conflict. It will have left you and you will be alone in your peace and calm. Can you stand it? Would you be able to face peace and no longer desire struggle and conflict? Would you be comfortable in peace? It is up to you....

❧

*A*s we begin to see how we are created by our beliefs, we will begin to look at some of our own beliefs to see how they have shaped us. We are now at a turning point, whereby we will be allowed to see more clearly how we destroy our own good in order to follow our own rules. As we learn to see how we are destroying our own good, we will begin to see the new belief system take over and allow us to receive our good. To receive 'good' is to allow it to be. You receive 'good' when you allow yourself to be in your good. To be in your good is to see yourself as good. Once you learn how to see how good you are, you will be able to see how good life is. You will begin to switch and to view all life as good. You will begin to know that you are in your right place, and you will no longer struggle to move ahead. You will appreciate you and you will love you. You will know you, and you will allow you to be free of restrictions and pain.

Once you let go of your need for restriction, you will begin to see how you are no longer being put to the test by you. If you begin to see your life as a gift with no restrictions, it will become just that. Until now you have been taught to expect to pay for anything you receive. You need not pay, and you need not feel like you owe. You tell yourself that you cannot have this or that, so that you might keep what you believe to be your high moral standards. You are not being moral, you are simply being "right." The difference between right and wrong was pushed at you from the time you were born. Let it be. You are not here to make rules to bind yourself up. You are here to be free.

As you continue to see how you have been making rules for you to live by, you will also see how your rules restrict and bind you. You will see how you feel imprisoned and trapped by these same rules. Once you can let go of your rules you will begin to tune in to your own intuition and guidance. You do not use intuition and guidance very often. For the most part you use your rules of what's right and what's wrong. You are going to move beyond rules, and you are going to become in tune, or in sync, with all of nature. Once you have tuned in, you will be surprised at how much you have been missing out on all your life.

If you begin to see through the eyes of love, you will not be able to use your rules. You use your rules to allow you to be good and morally right. Love does not depend on good or right. Love depends only on acceptance. If you can accept it, you can own it. If you can own it, you can decide what to do with it and how to use it or not use it. If you refuse to accept it, you cannot own it and you have no way to put it anywhere, because in the non-acceptance of anything you push it away. Once you push it away you create a detour in the energy field around you, and if you push enough away, your walls of protection are strong enough to repel all energy that is flowing towards you. Be it something you want or be it something you do not want, it will still be turned away due to your code of ethics, or your belief in what is right or wrong.

So; be careful what you believe and be careful about your morally right behavior. Those who have been hurt as a child may have particularly strong moral beliefs. Some of you hide behind these beliefs and try to cast your shame onto everyone else. You are not going to be allowed to carry shame into the light. The light will show it for what it is. Shame is a belief that you or another is bad or wrong. You are neither bad nor are you wrong. If you were shamed as a child, you simply took on the belief of those around you and your religion helped to enforce it. Religions like to teach you how low and awful it is to be human so they might teach how glorious it is to be God. God is in you, so how can you not be glorious too? You will begin to notice that as you begin to see love and let go of fear, you may not feel so strongly about religion. Your fear of religion is based on your fear of shame and guilt. You will let go of such heavy energy as you move into the light.

As you begin to know parts of you that were not available to you in the past, you will gradually begin to understand your past and how you have operated around these parts. You will begin to see how you have maintained certain rules to live by so that you might support the burying of these parts. As you let go of your rules to live by, you will allow your parts to surface and to heal. You are all healing on some level and you are all being born into the light.

As you learn to let go of your need to be in the right, you will begin to see that wrong is not so wrong after all. You will see that what you believe to be wrong was just set up in you to be wrong. You were, and are, taught the difference between right and wrong, and this may vary from person to person depending on your beliefs. It may also vary from person to person depending on your country, or origin of birth. As you learn to redefine right and wrong you may want to be afraid to set new rules for yourself. After all, rules have gotten you into some pretty tight corners with no way out. I suggest you go with the flow and not try to define everything in terms of good or bad. Allow everything to be what it is and you will begin to see how you are the one who creates stress by not allowing things to be how they are.

You will find that you change your situations by changing you. You will find that you begin to put you in a position of playing God when you decide how one should, or should not, handle a particular situation. You are not in a position at this time to play God. Allow God to lead his children, and you try to follow him instead of bring him up in your life. God is always here and present. You need not call upon him to be of assistance, you need only get out of the way and allow him to be of assistance.

Once you have gotten out of the way, you will find that you are the one with a problem. Creation does not have a problem. You have been taught to believe that you know best, and that you are wise when it comes to judging right from wrong. You are not wise in this area. You are ignorant, and out of this ignorance comes your desire to change everything outside of yourself. If you do not understand what is happening you get all upset and think that you must fix it or push it away. It is okay as it is. Do not play God, and do not push your will on others. They know the part that they are meant to play and they are acting it out.

If you allow yourself the time to heal, you will begin to see how everything is perfect. Once you begin to heal, you will begin to allow everything to be God. As you are now, you cannot allow for this possibility. You will begin to love you by allowing you to be, and you will begin to love life by allowing life to be.

As you learn to know your own ways, you will begin to see how you have actions which may create strong reactions in others. Once you learn how this works, you will no longer wonder why people react to you in a specific way. Once you learn to contain your ability to throw off charge, you will begin to see how you will slow down your reactionary parts. You will begin to see how you are set up as judge and jury and, therefore, you cause and create most of your own problems. You will find that you are learning about discharging these highly charged or activated parts now. This process is enema. It allows you to discharge and to activate areas in you that have been dead or playing dead.

Your enemas have a powerful effect on your entire body. They will affect your emotional body as well as your physical body. Enemas are discharging built-up, held-in poisons that are trapped in your cells. You are releasing your poisonous venom and you are releasing your charge. As you continue to take your daily enemas, you will continue to see dramatic changes in your physical body. This leads to an eventual shift in your mental as well as emotional bodies. As you learn to know more regarding how you function, and what your habits and beliefs are, you may want to thank you for having the sense to clean you out! After all, it does take time and blind faith to walk this path. You deserve a pat of the back and a great big "thank you."

You are saving you, and you won't really realize the extent of this statement for some time to come. You are being freed up from your past, and you are moving full ahead into your future. You are no longer going to suffer for your sins by carrying the guilt on your back. You are going to put down your burdens and follow God.

You are already in a position to free yourself and you are moving closer to total freedom. This will, of course, mean giving up all judgment and allowing everything to be. When you no longer have the urge or desire to show another how wrong they are, you will have given up your belief in retribution. You will have let go of your need to show the difference between right and wrong, and you will have decided to *allow* everything to be. This is peace. This is moving into peace and letting go of pushing others to be more like you believe they should be. You will have let go of your need to control others so you might feel safe. This allows you to let go of your fear. Your fear is based on not feeling safe.

Once you feel safe, you will create love and no longer 'fear' fear. You now 'fear' fear to the extent that you begin to lose your love to it. You will begin to embrace love by letting your fear surface, so you might release it. You will find that it is most easily released through enemas. The daily charge that builds up in your body can be easily discharged through enema and you will be allowed to take on light in the process. You are dealing with unknowns here, and the best way to begin to clear for the coming new world is this process of enemas. You will be happy you chose such a simple, inexpensive way to save you from slipping into total darkness.

Discharge what you can and release residue through the emotional body. Allow your body to scream if it must and allow your body to strike out or hit or kick. Pillows are great for this. A bed works well if you feel the urge to verbally (or physically) abuse another. You may feel the need to set someone straight in their crooked thinking, and this will only be you trying to change them to be more like you. Once you allow them to be who they are, you will be allowing you to be who you are. If someone does not like your point of view, it is simply you not liking their point of view. You start it and then you draw it to you so you might see what you have put into motion. Once you learn to stop fighting with your creations, you will have taken a giant step forward.

Once you begin to feel the part of you who is at odds with you, you will no longer believe that you are all bad. You will begin to see how you simply have a part of you who wants to tell you how bad you are. Guilt has been passed down and carried around for eons. Now it is time to let go of guilt. In order to do this you must begin to let go of your sense of right and wrong. Wrong is directly connected to guilt. Once you see how you use right and wrong, you will begin to see how you are going to be put in a position to be punished for anything that resembles wrong behavior.

You have set up a system within you that is judge and jury, and this system will always let you know when you are going against what you believe to be good. If you are bad, you will receive 'bad' from you. If you are good, you will receive 'good' from yourself. This is all done through your nervous system and through your brain. Your brain will produce symptoms that will tell you that you are not well, or it will produce insight to frighten you, or it will simply interfere with your normal thinking process. You have programmed yourself to be punished for bad, or wrong, and your brain obeys this programming.

Once you have let go of right or wrong, you will be letting go of your programming, and it will begin to relax and no longer punish you. As you let your programmed information slip into its own demise, you will be allowing yourself to be born again. You will allow a new system to be born in you, and it will run on trust and faith and will have nothing to do with judgment. Once you learn how to balance, you will be happy and you will see happiness. As this process of clearing judgment against the self continues, you may find yourself in a bit of confusion. You may also find that you are hurting and punishing yourself needlessly. This is self punishment leaving. You will see it as it leaves and you will know it, as it is very strong in all of you.

Once you have begun to accept yourself as good, you will no longer find it necessary to judge and punish you for anything. Once you know that you are in love with you, you will begin to treat you with kindness and with affection. You can tell if you treat you well by looking at those who are closest to you and how you treat them. If you are treating them with kindness and affection, you are more than likely treating you in this same way. If you simply tolerate them you may be simply tolerating yourself. Once you learn to see how you are tolerating, instead of loving and accepting yourself, you will begin to make room for love and allow tolerance to slip away. Now and then you will find that you begin to actually like being you, and this is directly connected to how pleased you are with your performance. I want you to love you regardless of how you perform or what you do. I want you to love you simply because you are divine. I want you to love you out of a need to be you, not out of a need to be good or right.

Love you no matter what you do, say, or think. Love you until you radiate with love. Love you until you are no longer afraid to be you. We have a very big problem here, and this problem is that everyone is afraid to be who they are. Your greatest fear is loss of the self through death. Your second greatest fear is not being accepted, and you are the one who is rejecting you. Once you learn to accept and embrace you, no matter what you are doing, you will begin to see how it feels to be love and light. You will find that you are at a turning point in your evolution, and this turning point is taking you within to show you how to transform into light. You need not remain in darkness. The veil is being lifted and the mysteries that blocked you are not so mysterious. You are simply not going to fear being you any longer. You are going to be you and to love you.

᠅

Once you begin to uncover various attributes, you will automatically see how you are coming forward, and you will know that you are no longer stuck. Most of what you do, or do not do, is programmed into you. Most of what you approve of was programmed for you by your association with your family and your civilization. Most of what you disapprove of was programmed into you by your family and your civilization. You are a walking computer that has been taught to react, or behave, in a certain way or pattern. Once you begin to break those patterns you will be upset with you. You will wonder what you are doing, and you will worry that you are being off-balance or out of whack in some way. You will wonder if you are being wrong in what you are doing because you will be breaking your own rules. You may not feel like you have control of yourself. You may feel that you are no longer in touch with yourself. In actuality, what you are doing is becoming more of you and what you naturally are.

You see; you are not naturally programming. Programmed behavior is not what you truly are. You will find that you are organic. You are not to be considered a programmed robot any longer. You are breaking away and you are going to begin to use your intuition and your creative power instead of your behavior patterns. You are switching from being a dominant force for integrated information, to becoming a dominant force for the light of creation. When you deal with information only, you lose your ability to sense things and to "know" things. You begin to categorize, and to twist things to fit into your categories. You are now going to allow things to be. By allowing everything to be a creative force, you automatically let go of creating forces that are destructive. If you see everything as a creative force with a purpose, then you lose your ability to see forces as destructive. You no longer have a destruction category and so everything falls under creative instead. This gives you a very positive outlook and lets go of your negative one.

Let's look at some examples. First of all, let's look at politics. Politics, in most countries, are very strong. You rule with strong governing and strong enforcement of your rules. Once politics becomes your central governing power, you literally feel controlled and manipulated by politics. Once you break away you will feel free. It is the governing over you by rules created to help you, and yet you feel helpless under the onslaught of all of these rules. This is programming gone astray. It started out to protect and ended up harming, or causing conflict. Once you learn to see how you create conflict by choosing to hold on to un-flexible rules, you will begin to see the benefit in letting go and letting God reign over your lives.

Government and politics are not the only areas of programmed un-stability. You also create problems within your private relationships, based on what you can or cannot accept as appropriate behavior. This includes friends and lovers as well as your children. You try to mold them into your specifications so you might feel safer and more comfortable with them. When they will not mold into your rules you begin to push at them to do better, which simply means (to you) to be more like you think they should be, according to your set of values and rules.

Once you begin to see how many areas of your life this affects, you will be horrified. You have spent your entire life judging and prejudging. This will all change when you move from programmed robot to creative force of God. You will shed your false beliefs and you will begin to live in the light of love. You will begin to know you as you truly are. You will become more you and less rules. You will become intuitive, insightful and psychic. You will know what it is to be a prophet and a visionary. Your life ahead is full of freedom, and your life up until now has been marked with fear and imprisonment. You are the prisoner of your own rules and beliefs. You may expand now and come out of this destructive process known as morality.

You will find that this system of right and wrong behavior is making many of you into victims, and to be a victim you will automatically find a villain to blame. When you play the victim, you no longer take responsibility for yourself and for your action, or your inaction. You get stuck in blaming someone else for everything that goes wrong, because you do not know that you are the creative force. How can you know this when you are so busy paying attention to right and wrong, instead of creating and owning it and loving your ability to create? Once you let go of judgment, you will feel free of punishment and pain. This will end your cycle of "an eye for an eye," and you will move on to create light and love based on fearless intelligence that "knows" without being programmed with rules. You are headed in a very powerful direction and you will be fulfilled, and you will create your own light and you will see how you are God!

Once you begin to understand the difference between fear and hate, you will begin to see that you do not hate much at all. The majority of you only fear to the extent that you cannot stand your fearful feelings, and so you project those feelings onto a person and you say, "I cannot stand that person." In reality, what you cannot stand are your own overwhelming feelings of fear.

As you learn to distinguish between these two different energies, you will begin to see how you can actually begin to heal both your fear and your hatred. Hatred is simply you being so terrified of someone, or something, that you simply must run or get away from the person or the situation. Hate is actually terror built up and blown out of proportion. Once you learn to see how you do not really hate, you will actually begin to give yourself a break, because you will understand that the part of you who believes that it hates you is only being terrorized by you. This is difficult for you to accept until you get in touch with all those parts who do not like or trust you, and you begin to communicate with them (these parts of you). So; as you learn to integrate you by allowing every part of you to come forward, you will actually be contacting your villain within as well as your victim within.

Once you begin to know these parts of yourself, you will begin to see how you can heal all of you simply by allowing all of you to be exposed. You fear exposure! You hate exposure! You are terrified of being exposed, because you truly believe that some part of you is awful or demonic. You are not! You only *believe* in evil. There is *no* evil. It is in the mind. As you begin to learn this truth, you begin to allow all parts of you to be exposed because you will no longer fear your unexposed parts, nor will you believe in their awfulness.

You are being taken on a ride here. You are being led into your own consciousness and you are looking at all levels of consciousness. The unconscious is simply a level of consciousness. It is an underlying level that is best left alone if you do not wish to ever touch your fears. If, however, you wish to touch and expose your fears, they will be found in groups in the unconscious mind. Many are presented to the mind in sleep state and many are never touched at all. From lifetime to lifetime they ride in you and affect your life and your decisions, and you do not even know you carry them. They are your fears and they literally rule your life from the unconscious. To bring them forward and expose them is to let them be in the light of day. In the light of day a big dark shadow simply vanishes.

This is how you will heal. Your unconscious is coming forward to be exposed. It does not particularly want exposure because it will then be seen for what it really is, and this will cause it to lose its hold over you. You are controlled by your fears, and your fears really want to stay in control and will fight to maintain their hold over you. You, in return, will want to give in to fear as it has always ruled you, but now things are about to change. You have conscious information that tells you to accept and allow, which is in direct opposition with fear which tells you to run and to fight against. Fear is about to lose, and the light of acceptance is about to gain control of every dark scary place in you – your subconscious!

So as you begin to clear your fears, you may expect strange dreams and situations in your life that will frighten you and make you feel like you want to run and get away, or maybe stay and fight. Try to stay in the middle. Try not to fight and argue. Try to listen. Try not to run and hide. Try to stand where you are and listen. Be quiet and listen. Do not hurt you and do not hurt another. Listen. Listen. Listen. Listen to your feelings and identify them. Listen to their feelings to allow them to be – accept them! Accept you! Allow you to know the truth by not finding right or wrong – no more sins and no more bad guy/good guy. Only love will be left standing between you and anyone or anything you touch. *Only love which is God!*

As you begin to see your own vulnerability you will wish to be kind and gracious with yourself. You are all vulnerable and you all have a fragile exterior. Once you become exposed you will feel fractured or, in some cases, broken. This will not last long. It is part of breaking up the old in order to create a new you. You will often find that you are no longer in a sense of humor, and you will begin to see how you can always regain humor when you need to.

You will also become aware of a tendency to frighten yourself with your own thoughts. This can effectively block you from seeing the good in any given situation. Once you have learned to let go of your fear and you come back into balance, you will see how you are no longer in need of fear. The desire to frighten yourself with your own thoughts will simply disappear, and you will be left with a desire to raise you up instead of put you down. As your thoughts begin to improve, your outlook on life will improve. Your output of thoughts will improve and this will allow your input to improve. Once you are putting out improved messages, you will clear the way to put in improved messages.

So; as out-flow gets better, it naturally will follow that the in-flow will improve also. What goes in then comes out, and what comes out circles and returns for recharging or acceptance. As you accept and allow everything to be, you actually give it life. You encourage its growth. What you block or stifle will go out and come back to be received. If it is blocked it will go around and enhance itself (or get bigger) and come back to be received again. If once again you block it, it will continue this process until it gets so big that it bowls you over upon its next return to you. It is yours! You projected it and now you refuse to own it as yours, and so it will get as big as need be to get accepted by you. Why? Because you are its creator. It is coming home and wanting acceptance so it might come out again as something new and different.

Do not be afraid to own your creations. Do not be upset when they come knocking at your door. It is your turn to accept and allow in order to change. It is simply the creative cycle. Allow everything to be and accept it as is.

❧

*A*s you grow in my light, you will become more accustomed to change. Change will no longer feel so upsetting, and you will begin to understand the importance of change. As you see how you have been stretched in one direction or another, you will begin to appreciate why you were stretched. Each time that you are stretched you are allowed to take on more light. You are allowed to see things in a new light and you are thus allowed to transform. I know how you hate change because you feel uncertain and insecure in it. It, however, is a great growth experience for you. You will find that as long as you can be flexible and change, you can become anything.

You are being transformed and it shows. You are changing genetically as well as organically. This genetic change is hardest. You have always been part of others in that you inherit traits, as well as beliefs, and even symptoms of illness. Once you have let go of your genetic programming, you will be healthier than your ancestors. Genetic programming accounts for a considerable amount of your behavioral patterns. One might exclaim, "Oh my, you have your father's expression," or, "Oh gee, she sounds just like her mother when she speaks." She may even think like her mother and not know it. He may act like his father or mother and never realized it. Genetic programming leaves an indelible mark on your cellular memory. Genetic programming is a source for most of your behavioral patterns, and it is in you big time!

So, as you begin to change, you will be thankful in most cases to remove the rules, beliefs, patterns and behaviors that your parents and their parents lived by. The rules of generations are passed down in some way. Usually it is through memory, and often this memory is in each and every cell of your body. The cells pass on what they know and you become what your past relatives believed, and this part of you is strong.

As you learn to clear and to release all problem areas in your behavior, you will cease your need to create problems for yourself. No more challenges will be required, and no more fighting will occur between what you are meant to be and what you were programmed to be. You will let go and you will release the past. This letting-go-of is change, and it requires you to change. You are no longer required to be who you were taught and told to be. You are free to choose your own beliefs, and, in doing so, to develop new patterns and habits and traits. You are not a prisoner of your genetic pool. You are going to rise above all that you think you are and you will become all that you really are. This takes time and patience on your part. You must be patient with yourself during these times of transformation. You will always be guided and you will always be cared for as you move into this age of becoming God or light.

It is very difficult for you to rise above the darkness. The low vibration feels more comfortable to you than this higher, faster vibration. You must, however, begin to develop within this faster vibration. This is what turns density to light, and the light is what you are. You are free once you are vibrating at a good speed and you will be allowed to go it on your own. Until you can maintain your own high vibration you will be supplemented with additional help. You will be lifted up if necessary, until you can keep yourself "up."

You are all rising up in this fashion, and it is simply a matter of time for each individual. It is also a matter of transformation from matter to spirit. You are stuck pretty deep in matter and pulling you up takes quite a bit of energy. The up-pull is as strong, or stronger, than the down-pull. This is what allows you to shake free of your roots and begin to rise to a new level within yourself. Once you have developed your own ability to pull upward, you will no longer require assistance. You will be in charge of your own ascension process and it will no longer feel like forced change. You will be pulling you in a new direction and this new direction will be "up."

Now; when you first begin to rise, you will find many new challenges. One of these is the ability to transform the ego from a small brutish force within you to a durable lasting assistant. The ego has been trained in reasoning out right and wrong, and now his entire job must change. You all know by now how ego protects and guards and defends at every turn. So, how in the world will you get ego to stop playing God and begin to flow and appreciate *all* of creation? The best way to handle ego is with kid gloves. Ego is out of control and believes he is totally in the "right" and in strong control. It is an issue of safety and not anger. The ego wants to keep you safe, and he believes that the best way to do this is to bully and to present an aggressive force to anyone who feels like a threat.

Right now, ego is so over-wrought with programming and fear that he can barely handle the least bit of criticism without feeling defensive. He is over-worked and anxious, and this anxious state is becoming hurtful. Once he is allowed to readjust to his role as provider of spirit, he will feel better. His original job was to show you how you are God, not how you are good or bad; right or wrong. He will happily accept his old job once he has figured out how to let go of his current defense position.

So, as you see the current changes coming into your life, do not be upset. Try to flow and try hard not to judge. You will see the benefit of living soon. You will begin to understand why you are here and how you are assisting creation. Once you begin to see this, you will be very grateful that you chose to come into matter and assist God in this little project.

⚜

You will begin to discover a whole new dimension to yourself once you have let go of your inner conflict. This dimension will be close to what you would call peaceful feelings. You will begin to calm down and not be so upset by things that occur. You will no longer be looking for the bad, or the push, in every situation. The push is usually right after you have been, or felt, pulled. The push is what you subconsciously do whenever you feel pulled.

Most of you have no recollection or identification with this conflict. You simply cannot identify with something that you do not realize is taking place within you. Some of you will get clearly in touch with this part of you, and you will see how it is against you in every way possible. Once you feel this part and recognize what it is doing, you will begin to know how you battle within you. This allows you to draw conflict, or battle, into your life. Once you are conflicted, your life becomes conflicted. You let go of conflict by using your ability to multiply your "positiveness" until it takes over. You can build a positive attitude by allowing everything to be good, and by looking for and seeing the good in everything. If this appears to you to be denial, it will show you how deep in negativism you are.

Once you learn how to be positive and how to recognize the positive, you will begin to change what has been programmed into you from century to century through the programming of your ancestors. As you learn to rise above these old belief patterns, you will begin to feel free of restriction.

Once you begin to feel free, you will be hit by the part of you who is afraid of freedom. This part will try to put you back in your right place which it believes to be "restriction." Once this occurs you will be fighting against a very big part of you, and you may feel exhausted and drained. You may also hurt yourself, or create accidents and illness, as a way to stop you from making the big mistake of giving up old rules and finding freedom in doing so. This part of you is afraid you will harm yourself by being free, and so it will punish you in a belief that punishment is the only way to keep you safe. It is much like a child who feels free enough to run across the street alone. The parent will spank the child, or hurt the child, to instill fear of crossing the street alone. You have a parent in you. There is a part of you who will hurt you to frighten you so you will not hurt yourself.

As you learn to deal with this part of you, who is convinced that it knows best, you will begin to see how you can easily be conflicted and how peace and tranquility can seem light-years away. In actuality, peace is right here right now. It's simply a matter of switching stations and becoming accustomed to the new frequency or sound vibration. You will enjoy peace when you learn to accept it. You will find it to be very direct, very safe, very uplifting and very happy. Peace is where it's at. If you want to be part of the newest fad it will be to jump on the "peace" mobile. Think peace of mind. Focus on peace of mind. Love and accept peace of mind. Let go of conflict by allowing for acceptance, and by knowing that all is well and good and positive. This will stir up all that is unwell and unhappy and negative within you. Once it is stirred up, or aroused, it will then begin to move up and out of you. You will see it or feel it somewhere in your life, or your consciousness, as you allow it to release and move out of you.

Do not be afraid of what is in you. Do not be afraid of you. Face you and allow you to be, and allow you to move and to change and to grow in light. It is not necessary to block what you think is bad because there is really no such thing. There is action and reaction, or cause and effect. This does not mean that any event that brings a specific cause to it was a bad event. It only means that you are learning to accept all 'as is' so that you might receive "all that is!"

Once you have become balanced you will know peace. Peace comes from your center and radiates outward.

Peace is the part of you who does not get upset and who trusts creation. Peace is the part of you who is in the middle in any situation. Peace is the part of you who is in your heart and connected to love. Peace will always seek out and find love. Peace will always know that all is well. Peace will hold you in high esteem and peace will allow you to hold others in high esteem. Once you know peace you will be allowed to know how to trust. Trust is built into peace and is a big part of it. You will find that peace is most often left outside of your life, and this is due to you being out of balance. Peace is in you, it simply has been buried under fear. Fear creates conflict and conflict creates struggle. If you struggle you are not going along peacefully. Struggle is 'not trusting,' and peace is 'knowing all is well.'

Once you find your center you will live a peaceful life simply because peace is at your center. Once you let go of your fear, which creates mistrust, you will begin to see how you are moving closer to peace. Fear and struggle are bedmates and wish to entangle you. Peace and love are connected in every way. You will know when you have reached your center by the amount of peace that begins to emerge in your life. You will find that, as you grow towards your center, you are actually moving upward. Your center actually vibrates at a much higher frequency than the rest of you. Your center is the part of you who is most you. Your center is where you will find your love as well as your light. Your center is the place in you that is most strongly connected to reality. Reality says that you are the creator, and reality says that you are God in every way. The lie sets up rules and operates from fear. The reality is that you, at your center, are God at God's center. You contain all that God contains, and God contains all that you contain.

So; if you are God, how can you not feel like God? How can you judge, and hurt, and criticize, and punish, and basically be big sinners who do everything wrong? How is it that you can be God at your core and judge yourself as not being God? In some cases you even judge yourself as being evil. How can this be if you are God at your center? You lost touch with God and began to be frightened by your lack of communication. You began to fear everyone and everything that you did not understand. Understanding was lost to you once you forgot how to communicate with God. You lost your connection so you felt lost.

You are not lost. You are simply disconnected by your own inability to see what is right inside of you. You are now learning to talk to God and to listen to God. It is no mistake that this series of books starts with a book titled *"God Spoke through Me to Tell You to Speak to Him."* It is all about reconnecting and communicating with your source, which is God. If you leave you unplugged, you will not receive the juice it takes to rise up to your proper level of awareness. If you do not reconnect to God how can you ever know God, or peace, or love? Peace and love are at your center, and this is where you will ultimately look for your answers. Plug in and tune in to God. "Light up" and know peace by returning to your center. You must let go of a great deal in order to reconnect, but you can do it.

You are now at a phase of your self-discovery that requires you to seek within and let go of looking for your answers outside of yourself. You will find that you are your best source of information and you are your best source of "light." Once you have reconnected, or plugged back in, you will begin to see big changes occur in your life. You will let go of your fear of knowing God and you will begin to know God on a very intimate level.

As you discover your way back to God in you, you will be discovering "peace." With peace, you will find joy, and trust will always be in your life. As you come to your center, do not be afraid to open up. You have been closed down for a very long time due to fear of lack. There is no lack. There is only abundance and more abundance. Get this cycle moving again in your life by receiving and giving. You will find that you do not belong in fear, and you will find your true pleasure in your center. Do not be afraid of pleasure. This is a time of great pleasure, and if you have been clearing and releasing your pain you will be ready, and you will have uncovered your pleasure which has been buried under pain and judgment.

☙❧

As you learn to recover your sense of peace and love, you will begin to see how joyful your life can be. You will find that you are no longer being asked, by you, to harm you in order to keep you safe. This in itself is a big step for you. You will begin to feel quite at home in you, and you will no longer be at odds with your own self. As this battle within you subsides, you will begin to see how everything has a purpose, and you will know that you are no longer being held back from becoming all that you are. There is a time and a season in the patterns of nature and natural evolution. A caterpillar should not chastise himself for not yet flying. He is in his crawling phase and will soon metamorphose into a bright winged butterfly. He will begin to fly when he is naturally ready.

Nature does not work by man's laws even though man, through his impatience, has created drugs to grow cattle and foul more rapidly than nature has intended. Your dairy products are spiked with enough drugs to require years of enemas to eliminate them. Your scientists are following your rules and trying to be "morally right" and feed the starving. Of course, money and financial gain is always a main priority and a great motivator. But now we come to a time of coming into sync with nature. You can best do this by being natural and by requiring yourself to follow natural ways. This means that you begin to take the "time" to evolve. A butterfly was not made in the day. It evolved from one state of being to another and it did so with grace. A caterpillar builds a cocoon and nests, and metamorphosis takes place naturally. Are you willing to stop and be still long enough for great change, or do you demand results now? How patient are you with you, and how long would you give God to show you things will be different before you give up and get upset? How calm and patient are you?

My pen has often exclaimed to her friends how amazed she is to still be writing this series of books. She began in 1988 and has had little compensation for her efforts, other than small donations and a life of "clearing" the physical body of fear. She has been pushed into "clearing" by her ability to channel this information. Her cells are pushed at and pulled by the struggle that is stirred within her by channeling such enlightening information. She is pushed at by her old programming and pulled up by her new "felt" enlightened programming. She has become a product of her channeling. As the information comes up out of her cells, she begins to vibrate it and to expose all of her life to what she is releasing in the way of light. She is igniting her own light and learning to operate from a new level of awareness. This level of awareness is what is inside of each and every one of you. You are actually enlightened beings but you have forgotten that you are coded with the intelligence of God.

Once you reach this intelligence which is inside of you, you will begin to transform "into" intelligence, or light wisdom. You are not meant to stay asleep and drifting. You are meant to wake up and know yourself (God). Know God. Be God. Feel God within you. Get in touch with your own intelligence, and begin to push out the darkness instead of pushing out the light. You can all get in touch with this part of you just as Liane has done here. Do you think that those who channel information at this time pick it up from outside of themselves, or do you now know that God and the universe are within and being reflected or projected out?

You are the one who will ultimately save you. You are God. You create it and you stage it, and you set you up to rise or fall. You may choose to fall in order to let yourself know that it is okay to fall. You may choose to rise up in order to show yourself that it is okay to rise up. You may wish to be in the middle in order to see how that affects you. It does not matter how you choose; only now we have all of you afraid, and fear is affecting your choices. Choices are no longer made from free will. Choices are now made from an imprisoned, weighed-down will. Will has gotten lost in itself and requires direction. Here is a clue for just you. Go within my child. Your answers are all within and your light is within as well. Talk to you. Listen to you. You have an entire series of books in you too and much, much more. Peace be with you and patience become you as you allow you to communicate with you!

⚜

You will begin to see a big change in how you relate to your outer world, and this will be due to the fact that you are now relating on a whole new level inside of you. Once you begin to see how change can be a good thing, you will begin to accept change more readily. Right now you are so afraid to be controlled, or told what to do, that you control others and tell them what to do.

Once you have found your center, you will no longer find it necessary to control everyone and everything. You will not be bothered, or pained, by things that now bother and pain you. You will become free to accept all of life as it unfolds before you, and its little twists and turns will no longer frighten you. You will begin to enjoy the ride and you will not fear it. You will begin to see how good and right "everything" really is. You will no longer judge and, therefore, you will no longer be upset by situations or people. You will begin to see how situations are created and not simply blocks put in your way by God to punish you. You will begin to see how you create certain situations so you might "let go" of certain behavioral patterns.

Once you see how everything is simply an opportunity for you to grow, you will begin to have a little more fun with your experiences. Once you can look at your experiences as growth opportunities, you can see how you are training and teaching you. You create it so you can live it and learn by it. Expansion is the name of the game. Taking on light allows you to expand, then you must draw new lessons and the lessons ultimately turn into just experiences without pain. Right now you are so dark and heavy that you feel a lot of pain with each movement closer to your center where the light pours forth.

You will find that, as you continue your move towards the center, you will be drawing more and more guidance to you. This is due to the fact that "light" carries all information that is necessary to become God. It is not becoming God in a literal sense, as you already are God. It is more of the realization that you are God. It is getting to know you enough to know who you are. Once you can stand in the middle of you, you will know you. The veil will have lifted and you will be exposed just like "Oz" in *"The*

Wizard of Oz." You will be so surprised when you finally "get it" and "know it" and "feel it." Now you only mouth it. There are so few humans who really "see it" right now, but in the future there will be many.

You are on a journey of self-discovery, and it is your way of convincing your judgmental mind and your strong will of who you really are. Without judgment you would automatically become bored and wish to return to your source. This task is the only thing that keeps you entertained and out of yourself. Once you have mastered this task, you automatically return to your natural state which is pure essence. Pure essence requires nothing and feels nothing. Pure essence is void of toxic matter. Pure essence is pure everything and yet it is nothing. The nothingness is you and you would freak out at that thought, so I won't shock you with it. You are going to return in the same fashion you went under – one step at a time, one layer at a time, one level of consciousness at a time.

This entire series of books is geared to your return. They are channeled in a specific order, and their order allows you time to slip into your greatest fears and gain insight as you do so. These books are being given so that you might return. This is set up by this woman who channels. She agreed to bring forth this information in an attempt to assist in the healing of souls. She is not so unusual. You too have a role to play. Some of you are simply here to follow and grow into consciousness, and others are here to assist and show the way. Do not confuse the pen with the information. She knows all of this information just as you do. It is part of her makeup, as it is part of yours. The history of lifetimes is in each of you. The history of God is "in" each of you. You tap into you and you will see. This is not always so easy to do. Do you know why Liane has easy access to this information? She set up her life pattern in advance (as you did). She also planned on being in matter and its denial and thickness. She decided that it would be necessary to learn early how to escape matter into the etheric realms, which you may call space and time, and which all of us now know are actually "within."

So she learned early to go within and stay for long periods of time. She learned that with the help of a dear friend. She asked this friend to do specific things to her in this life so she could access the inner realms and begin her road within. These things that were done to her set a great deal of judgment and psychological pain in movement as well. These things that were done to her are frowned upon and heavily judged and looked down upon. These things are considered abusive and frightening and monstrous and damaging and dangerous and extremely painful to the emotional, mental and even spiritual as well as physical bodies. These things are abuse and they served their purpose well. She was so terrorized and traumatized that she instantly went unconscious or within.

Now; here is the interesting part. Since birth is the unconscious realm, did she really go unconscious or did she go into "conscious" states. When you go unconscious is it really? Is there a difference between consciousness and being connected within, and the realms of outer consciousness that you think of as earth plane consciousness? Was she here on earth or was she in herself? Was she actually more conscious by being within herself than anyone who is outside of themselves might be? Do you know what consciousness is? How can you, if you are unconscious all of the time? Try going "within" to the conscious part of you. You have tried? Then maybe you need more trauma to assist you.

Now... I am not saying that pain and trauma are your answers; I am simply implying that you use pain and trauma in interesting and creative ways. Maybe you should stop judging it and allow it to be part of your plan. Some part of you knew when you came into this dimension that you would deal with certain heavy, mind-altering drugs. These drugs vary from money, to material gain, to achievement and social status. You also deal with drugs such as denial and escapism. You have much set in place here, and as the soul you know the blocks. You are "aware" in your unconscious or subconscious mind. Now you are going to become aware in your conscious mind, or *the part of you who is stuck in matter.*

❧

*W*e will begin today's writing by announcing that you have become very dependent on survival methods such as fear of hell. You have begun to believe that in order to survive and live forever in peace, you must avoid being bad and going to hell. Once you learn to overcome your fear of such disgrace and torture and banishment, you will be free to see what is really going on. Your salvation does not lie in avoiding hell and damnation, but you are so strongly programmed in this direction that it is difficult to release you. You will find that in Eastern philosophies you have your own set of concerns which are equivalent to a damnation story. Maybe your belief is simply that the soul never finds peace, or maybe it is doomed to return as a rodent or disgraced life form. Either way you are buying into a belief that says, "You'd better be good or else."

You will find that this pressure to perform is backfiring and creating some very big guilt on earth. To stop guilt you must stop judgment. To stop judgment you must let go of your ability to see everything from a right or wrong point of view. You must begin to see everything from within the context of creation. Creation fills the void and creation is part of the creator. Allow it all to 'be' and stop denying parts because you cannot accept them as good and right. Your judgments are based on ignorance of the creative plan. You have no idea what goes on inside of God. You barely know what goes on inside of you.

So; as you learn to grow beyond your belief in a punishing, revengeful God, you will be growing beyond certain limitations that block you and keep you ignorant. Another way to look at this is to see yourself as God and to wonder why you would create a hell, or a cycle of damnation. Once you see how you can create anything, you will begin to change what you choose to create. I think you will let go of this "eye for an eye" revenge thing, and I also think you will let go of this "frighten the children with big threats of damnation to keep them in line" thing. It works very well to keep fear going, but you are now moving out of fear, so why look for the worst when you can look for the best? Why see everything as bad, when you can have a central view that shows you all sides of everything?

So; in the big scheme of things you have been creating monsters to scare you, because you thought you could easily go out of control with all this "power-to-create" that you carry. You are breaking free of a very big lie now, and it will have huge effects on your consciousness and your ability to see clearly. You are going to bring heaven to earth as you let go of your need to frighten yourself with hell. You are going to own your power and no longer fear it. You are going to know how you are part of a giant creative force, and how you have the ability to shift and distort whatever you fear. You can create it and love it or you can create it and fear it.

Now; when you began to create your monsters and demons, you got so carried away that you forgot to give them love. You forgot that if you shift your perception a bit, you can see with understanding instead of confusion. Confusion causes you to "push." Understanding allows you to pull to you. With confusion you tear and separate, and with understanding you heal and bond to you. So; as you created what you judged to be ugly, you began to push it away. It felt this as rejection and so it pushed back. This was the beginning of war and struggle in creation. An energy that was seeking approval and acceptance was pushed at, and told how undesirable it was. This created many rifts and tears in the creative process. Now, all of a sudden, you think you have done something wrong. You don't know why your creation is ugly to you, and so you find this unattractive part of you to be quite disquieting.

You now have created separation in you. One part of you loves to feel the creative force that runs through you, and another part is afraid you are doing something wrong, simply because you could not see the beauty in your last creation. Years later you may have come to understand the purpose of such a hideous creation, and maybe you will want a second chance at accepting it instead of pushing it away. Maybe you had static in your magnetic field, and that static disrupted and impaired your ability to see things clearly.

So now you have set a whole chain of events into motion by pushing away a part of you or your creation. Once you have seen how this cycle works, you will know that there is no harm done. Everything returns to its source and so, eventually, your creation will return again. So; why get upset when you see it happen again? Why not embrace it and say, "finally you have returned."

≈≋≋

When you begin to raise your vibration, you will reach a point where you automatically begin to shake loose your old buried debris. This is similar to any vibration that shakes things up and knocks things loose. You will be vibrating so fast that you will automatically begin to clear and to release old stuck stuff. This will be, in some cases, how you knock down walls that you have built to protect you. These walls began as a protective device, and now they literally imprison you and keep you from receiving what is good and informative and even healthful and helpful. These walls are locking you in and everyone else out. You get to hide behind these walls that protect an out of date system. This system is part of you now and it must go. You will see many changes in your world as you begin to change you. You will see walls coming down and boundaries expanding and even merging. This is a time of great change and expansion. You are no longer limited, and you are no longer going to fear and blame others. When this fear of others leaves, you will begin to see everyone as equal and part of the whole.

Once you have begun to lose your boundaries by allowing everything to merge and flow as it was meant to, you will begin to see how certain boundaries have blocked you and stopped you from merging and becoming "one." Once you begin to merge within your own self, you will begin to see unusual changes outside of yourself. This merging within will begin to project new images outside of you, and you will begin to notice how your own personal world is changing and how it will flow once it is reconnected to the source, or "heart" of God. Once you reconnect, you will feel so calm and so peaceful and so loved. You will not feel afraid. Fear does not exist in the heart of God. You will find that fear only exists in the ego, and the ego is now waking up to his new identity.

Once the ego awakens he will "remember" his true identity, and he will give up this need to prove people wrong and to prove situations wrong or bad. Ego will stop blocking love and begin to receive love. Ego will try his best to hold on to his old job of blocking and protecting, but he will gradually become deflated and defeated as he begins to be flooded with energy that pushes him toward the light, which is the love that he so fears. Once he is pushed in the direction of love, he will begin to remember love and to enjoy love once again. His ability to *rejoice* will return and this will put him in *joy*. He has not felt "joy" in a very long time. He would not allow himself pleasure, and joy is a very great pleasurable "feeling."

Once the ego is gently pushed towards the light, he will begin to merge with the light and his identity will begin to merge with the light. So; what pushes him towards and not away from the light? Desire! Desire will allow the ego to move. The ego is very strongly connected to desire and less strongly connected to need. Desire is that part of you who really creates. Strong desire is a powerful force. So; how badly do you desire peace and freedom from what you now call your current identity? How badly do you wish for change in your consciousness? How much would you give up in order to receive? Will you continue to cling to the past programming that says, "social status is what makes you what you are," or will you be moved into the future where your new programming is saying, "God is what makes you what you are?" How far are you willing to go or stretch? Will you be able to go beyond your comfort zone to be God? Or will you stay stuck in your current identity?

Your "desire" to be the light will determine how far you will allow yourself to stretch and be stretched. Some of you will give up and wait for the next bus or train. You will not be able to handle the light if you are too fearful and desire is too weak in you. However, you will get another turn and you will not be left behind. The second team to rise up will be around the year 2020. The first team began to rise up around the year 1966. This will continue in cycles until desire for light (love) takes over completely and you begin to "see only love." At this time you will be vibrating quite rapidly and you will find it much easier to rise with the "B" team than it was to rise with the "A" team. The "A" team has the greatest blocks and energy shifts to deal with.

Once the first breakthrough is complete you will find it much easier to do a second breakthrough. The walls or blocks will have been weakened considerably. You will not require so much "pull" to get up and out of the darkness. You will see the light from the crack in the wall left by the "A" team. In many cases the "A" team will gently and lovingly guide the "B" team through. You will know how to do this if you are part of the "A" team, because part of your purpose is to be a "guide" for others.

Now; as you begin to break through and out of old molds you will see a lot of wreckage. Some of this may disturb you as you are not yet accustomed to the cycles of creation. After all, you are a very young, and just now emerging, consciousness. You are only at about five percent of your mental and spiritual abilities. You are just beginning to merge with creation and to trust the flow and thereby to open up to greater awareness and intelligence. So, once you open, you will use more than two to five percent of your brain. You will begin to accept "all" of you which means you will be accepting "all" of creation, and since you are God and creation is God, you will, for the first time ever, since you came into a body, be accepting God. Won't that be wonderful? It will have taken a few thousand years but you will have finally evolved into your true identity by simply accepting who you are.

⊰⊱

I am now going to tell you how you will begin to ascend. You will begin to rise at a very gradual, steady pace and you will begin to ascend as you rise. This rising up will be accompanied by a lifting up of spirit. Your spirit will literally rise in its position. You will begin to feel your spirit lift. You will begin to feel joy flow through you. You will begin to know heaven as you were meant to.

Now; here is the key for all you beginners and "A" team members: "Be patient!" Patience is your number one best friend. Patience will allow you the time that is required to release the weight that holds you down, and patience will allow your cellular structure to mend and heal once said weights are lifted up and off of you. You have carried many burdens for eons and now it is time to release them and allow God to take over. You are beginning to see how you do not create sin; you only hurt yourself which is equivalent to sin. You are going to learn how to rise above sin, and you are going to learn that sin does not really exist in the way you now believe in it. There will be no wrong and there will be no good. There will only be God. God feels good as you know good to feel. In reality good is simply an expression of a feeling just as bad is. Once you learn to see how everything you judge is simply based on how it makes you feel, you will begin to change your feelings and grow beyond the level of disliking or judging how you feel.

Once you learn that you create your world by how you "feel" towards it, you will begin to wonder why you feel so badly towards certain things. Could it be that something once occurred that was judged as awful, so now you "feel" things as "awful?" What would happen if you let go of all of your awful feelings? Would you no longer feel awful about anything, simply because you no longer had the feeling "awful" in you?

So, if you no longer had the feeling awful in you, would you then have other feelings to project onto situations – maybe the feeling of knowing or understanding or seeing with clarity? And if you have these strong feelings in you, would you be blinded by your feelings towards awfulness, or would you now understand every situation and know it occurs in harmony, and not resist it out of your knowing that it is simply part of what is being created in response to a specific action or reaction? And once you have this clarity of feelings, as well as clarity of mind, wouldn't you automatically "feel" better all of the time? And if the original judgment was created in the mind, wouldn't it be a good idea to change your mind first, since your mind affects and influences your feelings? And if you felt good all of the time about everything, no matter what, wouldn't that mean that everything was good and nothing was bad, only because you have been cleared of all bad feelings so you no longer know how to "feel" things as bad, you only have the good "feelings" left?

You get to decide how you will view creation by how you "feel." *You are in charge of Heaven and Hell.* You get to change channels and make it a disaster, or a beautiful fairy tale. It is all up to you. Creation is a gift, but you found a way to see it without "light." You began to call it dark and to "feel" dark towards it. It is not dark it is light! You are not darkness, you only think you are. I tell you how ignorant you are because that is where you have gone, but it is not who you are. You are not a pauper or a beggar out of a need to be. You went out of touch with you and can't find your way back to you. These books are written in a specific manner that may be displeasing and yet intriguing. They are leading you within you, back to you. You will find that not only are you giving yourself a gift by reading this material, you are also reconnecting you to the source of "all" inside of you. You get to experience a mental "shift" which will affect all parts of you. You get to reach into you and understand you, and this will lead you to see you.

Once you can see who you are, you will begin to "feel" you again. This will be a powerful move or change.

You will no longer blindly create, and then pout because everything bad or wrong happens to you. You will begin to "feel" your thoughts and desires, and know when to change in order to receive what is best for you. Until you understand how creation works you will not know what is best for you, so I suggest that you continue to trust God to create what will get you into an ascended state. You will find this difficult, because what most of you require is a good unloading of some very heavy energy. This includes judgments, fears, anxieties and physical as well as emotional (caused by mental) pain. Once you release these, you will begin to see everything from an ascended view. You will have clarity and you will know how to "feel" the good in you. This will take some time, but it is just around the corner.

❧

Once you begin to receive messages from your source, you will become confused. You have parts of you who have determined that the source is incorrect and creates problems. These parts believe the source to be a problem, and so they will object to your efforts to reconnect with the source of 'all that is.' Once you learn how to avoid conflict with these parts, you will easily accept the flow of your source. The avoidance of conflict is directly involved with how you act towards acceptance and how well you receive.

Your blocks will automatically block your source as well as create physical and mental and emotional binding. When something is bound, it gets plugged and over-expands with excess energy. Right now you have many such blocks in you, and you are constantly trying to quiet yourself with meditation and music and peace, and sometimes drugs and alcohol. Once you learn how to unblock you, you will no longer suffer from pressure build-up. You will no longer have these blocks so your energy will flow, and you will no longer feel pressured by your own self. This will dramatically decrease your need for stimulants and tranquilizers. You will begin to feel good all the time without your energy blocks. You will flow.

Now; once you have begun to flow, you will want to allow all parts of you to flow. This means you will no longer block your anger. You will acknowledge anger and allow it to tell you what is frightening you. You usually never get angry unless it is backed by fear. So, you will want to question your anger instead of giving it blind rule over you. You will find that you are quite often a frightened child, and most of your anger is due to old hurts and fears. Once you learn to trace your anger, you will see how it is not really anger it is fear. Fear hides behind other disguises and it will allow you, or even lead you, to believe that you are strong and right in your behavior and your attitude and your belief. Self-righteous behavior is brought on by such fear. Fear that is great is projected out as threats to another. If you are so afraid that you feel it necessary to protect yourself, you will begin to accuse those around you of not being smart enough, or at least not as smart as you.

Once you step into self-righteous behavior, you will begin to believe that you have an edge over everyone else and that everyone else is just too slow for you. This is an elitist type of behavior and it rules religion. Religion is based on the belief that you have just been privy to all the "right" rules of behavior and therefore you will learn how to be saved. Religion, as everything else, has its own agenda. This is not bad and it is not good. It simply "is," and it was created from the source, as "all" is created from the source. Once you begin to see how you use your self-righteous behavior to judge others as less than, you will want to bring it back into balance. Even those who read this information will begin to "believe" that they know more, or have greater awareness than others. I want you to realize that this information is more like a set of instructions, designed to bring you out of a place where you feel stuck and trapped.

In the beginning you all felt stuck and trapped because you went from being an expansive, all-knowing soul to being a tiny pin-point of light in a form. Form was and still is very new to you. You do not know how to be expansive and yet focused into such a tiny point of light. You will learn to balance your Godness with your humanness, but do not mistake this to be a one and only way. There are many ways! There are always many ways! This one is just the most effective for those of you who are drawn to these books. You may meet others who have been drawn to other ways that are just as effective, and your way is not more than or less than theirs. They are in their right place and you are in yours.

You do not know much from where you now sit, so do not be so self-righteous as to preach to others. We do not require preachers in this world. We do require students. Enough of you have been teaching your way for eons, now it is time to learn. Do not strive to be a teacher – strive instead to learn and to grow and to be of the light that is the source of all. You will know when you have reached the light because "everything" will make "perfect" sense to you, because "everything is perfect!"

***

Once you learn to know your own identity you will no longer be searching for something. Did you ever wonder what is missing from your life? It is you. Parts and pieces of you were pushed aside so that you could fit into a specific mold. Society and the rules said "this is how you must be." In youth you usually rebel, but, for the most part, you all began to adapt at some point. It is easier to play by the rules and to remain a good boy, or girl, than it is to always fight against what is pulling at you. You will find that, as you regain the parts of you who were dropped or pushed away in order for you to adapt and fit in, you will actually begin to feel better in certain ways. You will feel more whole and less in need of validation from others.

Your need for validation comes from being invalidated. You invalidate you by not allowing you (or parts of you) to "be."

Once you begin to accept the parts of you who were pushed aside, you will begin to feel stronger on some level. You will still feel the struggle that goes on, but you will no longer feel so incomplete and invalid. At some point you will actually begin to see how you have always been searching for you. You are searching for your lost freedom and your ability to create from an independent perspective. Individualism is a very difficult thing to define, especially for a species that is all "one." Once you learn how to live within the whole and yet play your part, you will see how the "whole" puzzle requires all of its unique and different pieces in order to show off its full potential or picture. You can have pieces of a puzzle missing and still see a picture, but the beauty of the "whole" picture is unmistakable and is a true gift.

Once you learn how to put all of your own pieces together, you will begin to see your own majestic beauty. You all have fractures and holes in you. This is a time for healing, which simply means looking at your holes and fractures in order to see what could be brought into balance. You are not bad or wrong just because you have spaces missing. You are simply coming together, and you are being told to look at your fears so that you might assist in accepting the parts of you that you are rejecting.

When you push at you, you create stress and you pull you apart. If you push at a weak point in a wall, you can effectively knock the entire wall down. You have knocked parts of you down without knowing that you have. You have destroyed and damaged you and you do not know that you have. The degree, or extent, to which you fear harm from the outside world, is directly connected to how much harm you have done to you. If you do not trust them it is due to your mistrust of you. You are always looking into a mirror when you look at others and the world you live in. How do you see your world? Is it separate and stressful or is it whole and peaceful? Your world is in you, and you will project whatever is in you onto your outer world or screen. You are only in danger if you are hurting and harming you. You create it all, and you create what you have been programmed to create. Let yourself begin to see inside of you, so that you might undo some of what you were programmed to do.

You will only be afraid to look at your inner workings to the same degree to which you are afraid of you. *Fear of the self is fear of God.* They are one and the same. Once you cross this hurdle you will be on the home stretch. Once you begin to see how you fear you and how you create everything, you will connect the two. "Oh yes, this is the part of me who has created everything; the good times and the awful times. How can I become friends with this part of me who has caused so much pain?" This will be your first reaction to this part of you. You will not wish to integrate, simply because this part of you will feel bad and opposed to everything you stand for. At some point you will begin to communicate and develop a relationship with this part of you. You will no longer run and hide from you. You will no longer push you away, and you will no longer search in vain for the something that is missing in your life. This, of course, means that you will no longer be fragmented, you will be whole.

Once you are whole you will see both sides of everything and you will naturally move to the center or middle. Most of you now stand on one side or the other because you have part of you missing, and so you are unable to easily see both sides and so you cannot see the good in everything, you mostly see one side and you call it bad. When you allow good to return to your life you will automatically be using both sides of you, and this will allow you to draw energy from good and bad and see it all as creation – and all creation as "love." This will be the point at which you will begin to enter your bliss. This is a state of euphoria created by balance. Balance allows everything to be "pure" essence instead of "fractured or "fragmented" essence. Yes you have two sides. Yes there is polarity and yes – this is good!

❧

Once you begin to see how you are made up of many parts, you will want to know all of you. You will begin to see how you can ignore parts, and, in so doing, allow these parts to not be part of you. Your consciousness is made up of many levels and layers.

Once you learn to unravel your knotted-up parts, you will see how you can use them in new ways. Often parts were, and are, interchanged in order to fill gaps that are being created by the suppression of certain parts. You began to change you by denying parts of you. Once you deny or refuse to acknowledge a part, it must be somehow replaced. Often you use parts, that are already so stressed (from being stretched), to fill in voided areas. Once a part gets too stretched and stressed it begins to lose its elasticity or flexibility. It begins to break down and eventually malfunction. This part then must stop playing all these roles for you in order to heal and regain its natural form. Once it has refused to play these roles of filling in voids, you will feel like things are no longer working for you. In actuality, things are beginning to work for you. Once you have sufficiently stressed a part, it will reach failure and it will automatically go back to its original role.

Once you begin to feel your system break down, you will not like it and you will fear the worst. Look at it this way; you are becoming what you always were meant to be, by allowing what you now are to die. This is death and rebirth on a spiritual as well as physical level. This is God being born in you. This is order and perfection coming into chaos and merging with it. This is the cosmos directing and guiding and orchestrating. This is a symphony in the making. When all is complete you will be amazed as well as pleased. You have not been so pleased and fulfill in a very long time. You will know your place and you will feel comfortable in it. You will have returned home after a long journey outside of yourself. You will have all the parts of you back in their proper place, and you will no longer put up false fronts in order to pretend to be what you think you should be.

You will know you and you will *accept* you. This will be a wonderful and beautiful time for you. You will begin to feel nurtured and loved, and this will be you accepting you and nurturing you. All parts of you will begin to shift into their proper role. You will no longer push some parts away to be replaced by others. You will begin to see how you are being held in place in order to achieve this step in your evolution. You have all been held in place in order to get this far, and now you will begin to feel this support. As you open to new levels of this support, you will be adding to you. You are constantly recalling parts of you by simply becoming unsure and insecure. When you are unsure and insecure you automatically call for assistance. You usually hate feeling unsure, but it is at these moments that you draw on your support system. This in turn tells your support system how much it is needed, which allows it to stay in place. If you did not need it, why would it hang around?

So; do not be afraid to feel your vulnerability and your insecurity and your un-sureness. They add to your life, as does everything in creation. Do not judge anything until you know what you are doing. Right now you do not know the truth.

Once you begin to see how you create everything you feel and experience, you will begin to understand how you might be a little upset with you. As much as you know about you would fill a thimble. You know so little about how you are made up of thought, and how that thought influences every waking and sleeping moment of your life. You are a thought in motion. Which way are you moving? Who are you moving towards? Did some part of your thought decide to return to God? Are you being returned to God and does that upset you? Did you get so involved in being separate, and having your own identity, that now you no longer see any reason to pay homage to God... your creator... your other side?

What if your creator wants you to return? Do you think that you know more than your creator or the field from which you sprang forth? Do you think that you are so intelligent that you can judge these times as terrible? When you left, you did not plan on never returning. Did you know that you planned to return so you might recharge and remember? Did you know that you are not losing everything, and you are not having everything taken away in order to punish you? Did you know you are holding on to anchors that will not let you return? Some of these anchors are actually patterns in your energy field; others are simply behavioral patterns from other lifetimes. Did you know that sometimes you punish yourself, or make yourself feel pain, when there is really no need to feel pain? Did you know that you fell into agreement with pain and decided to let it rule over you next to fear? Did you know that all pain is illusionary and does not exist? Did you know that (on some level) you actually decide, "Okay, I will let this be a painful event in my life" or, "Nope, I'm not going to punish myself with pain on this one?"

Did you know that you can live without feeling pain? Yes, I know that I have explained pain as a signal, but what if that signal only lasted for two seconds and was gone? The role of pain in your lives is about to make a drastic change. Once you have cleared pain you will no longer use it against yourself and you will no longer hurt. You are about to see how you create pain, and this will allow you to see how to un-create it.

Now; I know you are all going to scream at me and say how you know pain is real because you are constantly in pain... be it physical, mental, emotional or just confused pain, it is very real to you. You will learn to let go of your *belief* in pain as a deterrent from bad behavior. You have used pain since the beginning of time and it's time to "let it go." So, as we continue this series of books, we will be focusing on what you create and why you first began to create it, so that you might make certain decisions and choices to let it go and return to God. Do you really want to keep this separate identity that you have created, or do you want to return and let go of all the illusions that were necessary to keep you from knowing God?

Let it go! Let it all go. Everything has a purpose and it will eventually move to become God. Everything is moving and stretching towards God (light). God light is it! God light is everything that is. God light will enfold you in peace, and God light will show you the love you so desperately search for in your lives. God light is the answer. You are close to finding it. You look for it in others, and you try to hold on to them in order to hold on to God light. You can find it closer to home. You can find God light in you. You are God light too. It is in you.

When you own your own light, you will stop looking for it in others. This will take a while to catch on because you are so trained to look at others for certain things. This is a time to look at you for what is in you and to appreciate you and to give thanks for being you. Just think... once you find your own God light, you get to feel "in love" all the time! Life will be a joy! Life will return to bliss. The Garden of Eden is alive and well. I never ran you out of town. You judged a situation and created a penance. You have used judgment and penance ever since. Guilt, pain and shame are man-made creations, and it's time to let go of what you have been creating and come back to God and his creations. You'll like God... he's a great ball of light and he's crazy about you. As a matter-of-fact he's asking you to please come back. He misses you!

❦

Once you begin to reconnect with lost or pushed away parts of you, you will begin to calm down and feel secure about who you are. You will no longer feel so small and fragmented. You will begin to feel whole and complete and trusting of the self. With this trust will come some very subtle but strong urges to be more or do more. This will be the part of you who is returning, adding its energy to the whole. As you learn to deal with your new levels of energy, you will begin to see how you have always searched for these parts and what they can add to your life. This new energy is not like the zing. The zing, that keeps you moving in the direction of excitement, is directly connected to fear of fear. The zing is more of a thrill-based energy. This new found energy will be stable and gradual in its build. It will not propel you from here to there; it will guide you and focus your attention in specific directions.

As you learn to deal with this new wholeness and the integration of you, you will begin to calm down and float instead of constantly believing you need to paddle your boat to get anywhere. You will plug into the flow more readily because your wholeness is parallel to the energy source. As you become whole by accepting all parts of you back, you will become identical to the whole of creation. You will be complete, and your energy patterns will match up to those of the whole of creation and you will automatically be drawn into it. Like attracts like in nature and in creation.

Once you have the right ingredients, by simply allowing all parts of you to return, you will be a duplicate model of your creator... like father... like son... like mother... like daughter. The creator has both female and male energy and so do you. You will learn to balance the yin and yang of you; and you will learn to accept the parts you have pushed away by judgment and dislike of, or towards, them. You will like all parts of you and find the good in them. Everything in you is perfect in the eyes of the creator. Creation's only problem is directly connected to judgment placed on it. It does not do wrong. There is no wrong way. It does not do bad and nothing bad ever occurs. Get that and you will have the secret of the universe.

Everything is and everything is okay the way it is. You do not decide what is okay and what is not. You are here to enjoy creation, and how can you enjoy something that you continually find fault with? You are here to enjoy God, and how can you enjoy something you continually find fault with? You are here to enjoy you, and how can you enjoy someone you continually find fault with? Where is your enjoyment? It is in money. It is in relationships. It is in new homes and shiny cars. It is even in drugs. Can you not share some of your enjoyment with yourself or with God or with creation? Why must you always be on the outside of enjoyment? Why can't you just enjoy having and owning "you" like, or in the same way, you enjoy having or owning money or a mate or a shiny new car? Why can't "you" bring you as much pleasure? Did you lose something important along the way? Did someone forget to teach you the joy of ownership that comes with owning you?

You are a "one-of-a-kind, not-two-like-it in the whole world of creation." Does that not make you very valuable and even a collector's item? How will you care for this valuable item? Will you judge it and find flaws in it, or will you treasure it and enjoy looking at it and touching it and holding it and learning about it? It is time you begin to appreciate you so that everyone else will begin to do the same. You send out the message "do not appreciate this messed up piece of work" and everyone picks up your message. You can change your message by accepting all parts of you and by appreciating all parts of you.

❧

Once you begin to integrate, you will begin to feel satisfaction within yourself. This satisfaction will be due to the gratification you are feeling from accepting some major parts of you back into you. You have always tried to disown the parts of you that you do not like. Most of these parts are behavioral patterns, and some are dysfunctional now from being pushed away for so long, but these dysfunctional parts will begin to find their correct patterns and operate at a new level of intelligence. You will find that, as you learn and grow, all parts of you also learn and grow. You get to help unconscious-to-you parts as well as conscious-to-you parts. You will begin to see a pattern in your life. This pattern will show you how you operate.

Once you learn and grow, your pattern in life will automatically grow. You are gaining insight and teaching yourself a new way to view reality. The teaching of the self is what expands the self into any given direction. Once you have grown a little in a new direction, it will be easier for you to go a little further in that direction. Then, once you get a good portion of you moving in that direction, you will build a momentum that will assist the rest of you in moving also.

You will find that you are like a train that is being pulled by an engine. All the parts move because the engine is pulling them. The momentum keeps them going, and if the engine were to stop quickly, all the cars following the engine would eventually crash into one another as they hit up against the stopped engine. This is a chain reaction or a cause and effect event. Since you are following you, you can avoid further fast stops by moving more slowly. I have tried to assist you in slowing your life down. This is not because you need to get out of the fast lane to stay safe and well. It is more because you are all changing direction, and this switch in direction will be less painful if you have gotten off the fast track. You do not do wrong by living in the fast lane, but you do have certain complications that are directly connected to such a life.

As you learn to reconnect with certain aspects of your own nature, you will be giving yourself a big gift. Once you can uncover your hidden fears and confront your reasons for being afraid, you can literally transform your fears into assets. You can begin to grow with your fears and through them. Up until now your fears have been outgrowing you and keeping you hidden under their shadow.

When you allow yourself to stand face-to-face with your fears, you will be overwhelmed at the amount of power they have over you. You will feel your emotions upsetting and crashing off the walls of you as they try to adjust to big fear. Your emotions are so traumatized in some cases that you literally must communicate with your emotions and tell them they will be okay. Certain aspects of your nature have never been allowed to express, and for them to now express even the tiniest bit of feeling will be completely against their programming. You have been programmed to shut down certain parts of your nature, and you did an extremely good job of it. Now you are going to open parts of you up so they might add to your life, and this will feel very different for you.

Now; as you get in touch with these parts of you, you might want to suppress them again. After all, your programming has kept these parts down all of your life, and this programming is habitual at this point. You will, however, begin to loosen up and let some part of you bubble to the surface. As these parts come forward you will gradually learn to accept them and embrace them. These parts have probably never had your acceptance and love, so they will be cautious around you and they may want to hide and return to their dark corners within you. This will not last long, and eventually all parts will come into the light of day so that you might see who and what you are.

Now; some parts will have problem areas. You have huge tears and gaps and splits in you. You have created so many false parts (to replace the real parts that you judge as bad) that you will find you are splitting at your seams, like an old rag doll who has been tossed on the floor a few too many times. These tears and splits and gaps will take time to heal. My pen has just gone through a six month period where she could do very little as she waited for a rip or tear down her right side to heal. She is connected to her center (God) enough to see what she is healing. This gives her patience to not take drugs and to *wait* for the tear to heal. Some of you will have little to no patience with a six-month healing. You have not spent sufficient time communicating with you. You have not dedicated all of your time and energy to you. You will find that you dedicate your time and energy to whomever is most important to you. Who does your time and energy go to? Who do you love the most? How do you get you to love you the most? This is your trick question.

Many of you use pain to bring you back to you. Your attention immediately returns to you when you are in any kind of pain, be it mental, physical or emotional. Even made up pain works for you. You, however, are going to learn to dedicate you to healing you. No one else is going to do this one for you. You created it and you can un-create it. Your desire to feel joy will lead you out of pain. Your desire to be whole will lead you out of fractured beingness, and your desire for God will lead you out of the illusion and into heaven. Once you have gotten in touch with you, you will begin to have a one on one relationship with you. Once you have spent some time alone with you, you will be ready to spend more time in that direction. Remember, once you get headed in a certain direction it is easier to continue in that direction, as you will build momentum as you go. Welcome to your new direction in life. You are now heading "up."

As you begin to acquire enough energy to plug into your own source, you will begin to feel as though you are in charge. This will not be in an ego centered, controlling way but it will be with a sense of dignity and respect for the power you carry within you. You all have the ability to tap your own power source, but you spend most of your time trying to tap power sources outside of yourself.

I am going to tell you a secret now. You all think that there is some great mystery and purpose for life as you know it. It is not such a big deal actually. You got stuck here by your beliefs that you are part of matter and now you are getting unstuck. You believe life, as you know it, to be holy somehow and worth holding on to and protecting. You are "holding on" to a big load of matter. You can let go of it and remember that you are the energy of which this matter is created, or you can continue to be unaware and stuck in the middle of a big rock or blob of energy that has solidified. Come out of this game that you play. We are not here to distract our attention away from and out of us. We are here to focus on us, so that we might free our attention to return to its source.

You are not here to become one with the earth or with one another. You already created them so you already did that. You are only here to unwind and undo what you have done, because you went as far "out" as you could, until you lost so much of you that now you are in tiny pieces and you barely exist. Stop looking for you in another. Look for you in you. You are all "in" there somewhere, and the only thing that creates a block to you seeing all of you is your lack of enthusiasm for looking at you. You prefer to look at others to make you feel good and to make you feel loved and appreciated, and all the time it is your love and your acceptance that you are looking for.

Once you begin to actively search for you inside of you, you will discover your twin soul and all other parts of you who you actively search for in another. You are not lost to you; you simply have little to no interest in you. You could care less about you. You would give up your life to save your child or a loved one, but few would give up their life to save their own self. The self is lost to you due to lack of interest. The self is the soul of you, and you are so busy looking to what you can gain outside of you that you find what is inside of you to be worthless and unacceptable, especially if you have a choice between a mate or a new car or big money. You and what is in you is very unappealing when compared to such needs, wants and desires.

I will tell you now that your desire creates for you and you got into matter by your desire to create more, but you did not know how much of you would solidify and densify. Now you are screaming in pain because you are so stuck in the solid mass that you created out of your free-flowing energy. What will make you free and flowing again is to come back to spirit. Can you desire spirit over toys and relationships? I do not intend for you to give up matter altogether, but just enough so your major strength lies in spirit so you can be led by spirit. Spirit is freedom. Solid mass is confinement. Where do you put your energy? Do you put it into getting another to accept you, to love you, to appreciate you, or do you put it into you, where your source is.

I will tell you now that this transition, from without to within, will not be easy if you have a lot of you attached to people and things and beliefs that lie outside of you. You will find that the easiest and gentlest way to retrieve your spirit is to back out of the outer world and move inward. This is against everything you have been taught, and you still want to cling to manifestation with your life. You created a toy and you thought it was you. You are the creator. You created a game called relationships and you thought the game was you. You are the creator. Step out of the game and step out of the toys so that you can see what is really going on.

Now; I know how I have told you that in relationships you will experience you, and you will get those buttons pushed that require pushing in order to show you who you are. Now I'm taking you one step further. Drop out of relating to others and begin to relate to you. Do not make how you act with another your primary concern. Begin to make how you act with you your primary concern. Do not try to get them to like you; try to get you to like you. Do not try to get him or her to love you, try to get you to love you. Be with you when you feel the need to be with someone. This is really what that need is all about anyway. Do you get lonely easily? This is a clear indication that you abandon you big time. Do you feel rejection often? This is a clear indication that you reject you. Do you not trust others? This is a clear indication that you do not trust you.

Begin to know you so that you can love you. Here is a little secret for you to know: did you know that you will distract you from getting to know you by creating blocks to keep you apart from you? Some part of you will create distraction, in the form of whatever appeals to you, just to keep you apart; separated; fragmented. For some these distractions come in the form of drugs of all kinds, usually actual drugs such as alcohol, nicotine, sleeping pills, pain pills, caffeine, sugar rushes, food binges, work binges, excitement binges of all kinds. Usually the last thing anyone does is to sit still at any given time. You have to go, to do, to move, to create.

I want you to stop! Put the brakes on now... you are creating out-of-control. Just stop for a while. Give it a rest so you can undo what you have done. Stop creating more until we can clean up the messes you have already created. You have gone hog-wild and now it's time to slow the party down so things can become "peaceful" again. You don't have to be on the go every minute. You don't have to have someone to love, and you definitely do not have to have someone love you. Look at who and what you are... it is time now!!

Now; when you first begin to heal your split or bring together the two basic parts of you, you will begin to find your balance. Balance comes from accepting all parts of you. There really is no darkness you know? You create a dark reality by hiding parts that you simply cannot accept. Once you can learn to accept everything you will see how everything is light and love, and it is only your fear of something that causes you to push it into a less than light status. As you learn how to accept all of creation and to come out of judgment, you will no longer see a killer as bad and you will no longer see a child molester as bad. You will begin to see how everything is really created, and this will force you to accept that you do not have the correct answers to creation and how it works.

Once you begin to balance, you will see the balance in life. You will also see the places that are out of balance, and you will be able to accept them as simply out of balance places, instead of pushing them into a dark villainous role. You are all out of balance because you have all played the role of abuser in one life or another. You have all killed and been killed, and you have all molested and been molested. Your direct energy connection to these events in past life will determine how you react to the same situations in this life. If you hate someone for killing or bombing and maiming others, it is pretty evident that you are stuck in your victim role from having such pain inflicted on yourself in another time. If you do not mind killing and would gladly kill off a few folks who you believe to be evil, or upsetting to you, it is evident that your killer energy is still strong in you from another time.

So now we have you playing a victim and wanting to end suffering for other victims by punishing the hell out of the villains. You then feel better after the bad guy gets his just rewards, or your revenge. Now we have created an interesting cycle of imbalance. Not only are you the killer and molester (from past lives or this life), you are also the one being killed or molested (in this life or a past time).

So; who do you root for... the victim you are or the killer/abuser you are? Do you get the idea? You are damned if you do and damned if you don't. If you take sides, you lose part of you by judging it and condemning it as wrong; bad; evil; not good enough to exist. In actuality this is simply an imbalance in your energy field that will be corrected once you let go of both extremes in life.

Stop praising good and condemning bad. You are giving 'uneven balance' life within you. You are what you believe, and you are raising your victim level to new heights and pushing your villains deep within you. Find your balance please! Stop playing this silly, childish game. Know that you can kill and not be evil. You have all killed. I don't care if you are playing the role of a saint in this life, you probably chose this role to outweigh the sins you believe you created somewhere back in time. The key here is balance. Let go of evil! Come home to God. God is in your center. Let go of your struggle to be one way or another and simply "be."

❧

Once you begin to see how you have split into many compartments within yourself, you will realize how parts or pockets of you exist within you in a separated state. You may even carry pockets that have information for you. Some of you will channel this information, and some will simply release it when the time is right and you are ready to give it up. You may also carry a pocket of pain. This could be physical pain that was suppressed so you would no longer see it or feel it. If you release a pocket, or part of you who carries physical pain, you will begin to feel much better once it has been drained. You also have pockets in you that contain emotional pain, and these often bubble to the surface in a flash of emotional energy.

The other most common type of separated package within you is mental pain. You change what you cannot understand and you turn it into fear and distrust, and you are very, very full of these mental pockets. They rule you, and they cause you to be lopsided and pushed out of shape. Whenever you begin to release your hold on these pockets you will know, because you will get all excited and upset and bent out of shape over something. Just calm yourself down and know that you are releasing mental energy. Even though it feels emotional and has emotions behind it, it was mental judgment that created this pocket.

Now; when you begin to see this type of release you will want to be very gentle with yourself. Know that you are releasing and know that to release any kind of pain, be it physical, mental or emotional, is a good thing. Begin to watch and see how you draw situations to you to assist you in your release, or the "button pushers" you draw to you when a "charge" is ready to let go of its hold on you.

You will find that most often you do not create very big traumas until you are in a good position to handle them. Of course, you usually do not see this until after you have released and cleared the pocket or fragmented part you are working on. Where do you think garbage and brainwashing goes? Once you have been taught something it is now "in" you, and to release it, or release you from it, you must be untaught. To un-teach, you must bring it back up and out so you can rearrange the belief system. A good way to do this is to re-experience what you were taught so you might begin to see how you no longer need to carry that belief. Once a belief is lodged in you, it takes something bigger than it to move it.

So, if you do not wish to see big trauma in your life, you may never un-lodge your biggest fears and false beliefs. If you are willing to face you, you can begin to clear and release many lifetimes of debris and this will allow you to change and to grow, or transform into something much lighter than what you now are. Do not be afraid to look at all that you are and all that you carry. You are made up of many things, and you want these things to stay still in you so you will not have to feel them or to acknowledge them. Well, I am sorry my friends, but what is in you is creating you and your future. If you really want to keep it "still" and "quiet" in you, so it can continue to be a silent partner who creates things for you (that you do not know or realize are being created), you may continue this practice. All you have to do is say "do not move. I do not want to feel anything that I see as bad" and voilà it is yours to keep forever.

Now; if, on the other hand, you do wish to face all of you, so you might consciously know you and lighten your load, I suggest you begin to say "please heal me, show me love." This will do the job nicely. Mostly because what has been put in you lifetime after lifetime is not love but self-hatred. How do you see love when you are so full of self-contempt and self-loathing? You do not. What you will gradually see is loathing of life, and God, and the universe, and your neighbors, and anyone else you can find to project your own self-loathing onto.

Do not be upset with you for clearing and releasing the emotional pain that you carry. It is not yours to keep, and the longer you try to shut it up, or push it down so you won't have to feel emotional pain, the more confused you will get and the harder it will push to move forward.

Once you ask to become enlightened and transformed you will begin to transform. Again you start to judge this process and believe you and your life are a mess. You have "always" been a mess, and now you are cleaning up your mess so you can be what you are meant to be. Do you think you are being punished and that is why you feel your feelings? You are wrong. Yes! I said wrong! Pain has been a big part of you since the original split from God. You cannot even begin to comprehend the number of painful memories, from painful experience, that you carry from the beginning of time. Now you expect to zap yourself into a new state of being without feeling anything you are so full of. What you are most full of is pain! Pain from being hurt, pain from hurting others, pain from guilt, pain from judgment and, most of all, pain from being confused and believing that you are a victim. You are not a victim! You are playing a victim role if you think that you are.

As you begin to feel your pain, do not try to stop it. Allow it to move forward and out of you. Pain does not belong inside of you. If you keep it, by asking it to not make its presence known to you, it will continue to act as a magnet for you. Pain can only draw more of the same to you, so I suggest that you begin to move it and heal, rather than suppress it and allow it to grow bigger. You get to take an active role in your salvation here. Do not judge yourself for doing so. Congratulations to those of you who have been dealing with unwanted parts of yourself. You are truly Gods!

❦

Once you begin to see how you are fragmented you will know the effects of denial. When you choose to open to specific energy and close off to others, you automatically create a dramatic shift in energy. This shift causes you to lean to one side or the other, and you can no longer stand in the middle. You lose your center. You become tilted or off-center. To become balanced you must look at where you are off-balance, and then let go of your judgments. You all judge pain as bad and awful, so you all have denied pain in you. This pain is both emotional and physical, as well as mental.

Some of you will not want to look at your pain. If your denial of pain is very big, you will begin to doubt your own path. You will not think it is spiritual to touch pain. You will believe it is evil, and you will question or even stop questioning this information, depending on your level of denial. If denial is very extreme, you will not allow yourself to go any further with this information, and you will turn off to it in an effort to protect yourself from what is inside of you. You do not wish to stir up old buried pain any more that you wish to draw pain to you that is new. This pain that is buried in you is part of you. It acts as a growth or appendage, and it acts as a part of you. In some cases it is creating for you on many levels. It is often the part of you who you call avoidance. Pain is the part that directs you to avoid certain situations, and certain people, and even certain goals.

Pain has a very big hold on you and you are very much embedded in pain. Pain is a big magnet that draws daily inconveniences to you. Little things that go wrong during your day, and many upsets, are drawn to you by the magnetic pull of pain. Most of you have huge amounts of pain stuffed into various corners of yourself. Once, you used this pain to warn you as to when you might be getting too close to a painful situation. Now this pain simply thrives on its own and on the new pain energy you draw in with its help. Without this pain you would have pleasure, joy and peace within.

You will release your pain when you are ready and some will be ready before others. For each of you it will feel different, depending on how you have used pain and how many past you's are involved. You have all set yourselves up as judge and jury and you all hand out punishment. You each have your favorite way of punishing, and it varies according to how you seek revenge on yourself. You can tell how revenge filled you are by how desperately you want the bad guys to get their punishment. If you want the politicians pulled down from their high status and publicly embarrassed, it is a reflection of how you punish you. If you want the guy, who beat and killed his wife and children, to be dragged through the streets behind a car and then publicly assaulted, it is how you would seek revenge on you.

I have told you repeatedly that you are your own worst enemy. You create everything that happens to you, and then you sit back and cry and scream about how mean God is and how mean life is and how awful the universe is. You are God. You are life. You are the universe. It is all you doing it all to you, and you don't even know how you work. You know more about how your machines work than about how you work. And you know what's really ironic about it? You don't want to know... some part of you does have an idea that it's you creating reality, but you think if you can stay in denial you won't have to deal with "you." You don't like "you" and you don't even know "you." You see that one reflected back at you every day, don't you?

So; how am I going to get you to want to know you? We've gone through the positives to get you unafraid enough to look at the negatives, but how do we get you to "want" to clear your pain? How do we get you to look at it and *"feel"* it long enough to move it? How do we get you unafraid of this part of you? How does 'God on high' get 'God in matter' to realize that he is holding on to energy that must be moved in order to reunite with 'God on high'? How do I convince you that I am still God and you are still God and this is not a new punishment, it is actually salvation and freedom from pain??? How will we do this......?

⚜

You will find that you are quite full of holes or pockets of energy. You might call them dark holes in space, only you are the space. As you begin to tap into the spaces within you that carry your old, discarded and yet held on to pain, you will want to be very patient with yourself. Do not give you a bad time over the fact that you are now on a healing path. This healing of you may take you into many unhealed parts of you, and you will know it is you when you re-experience what is stored there.

Once you can allow all parts of you to release, they will automatically become useful again. This will allow for the separation to end, and you will find these newly cleared areas most helpful in creating a bright future for you. These areas have always had a strong hold on you; they simply worked against you instead of for you. You might see them the same way you would see a wounded leg. You have to hobble on a wounded leg and drag it along with you. A healthy leg is not only no longer a weight to carry, it also assists you in moving on and it supports you.

Your wounds hold you back. Do not be upset when you stop and take some time to heal old wounds. They come from old pains and old injuries to your psyche. You are healing you every time you allow feelings to express. Feelings include those you call painful. You allow them to be there for two seconds and then you get very upset with them. How can a painful old wound heal if you refuse to feel it? How is it that you have become so afraid of pain? Could it be that you do not realize how pain is actually a friendly signal, created by you to assist you? Could it be that through the ages you have made this part of *you* your enemy? Could it be that you hate this mechanism in you that was once so helpful to you? Could it be that you have made a very big enemy within you; and could it be that now is the time to end the war that goes on inside of you with various parts of you?

I am not asking you to hurt yourself or to live in pain. I am asking you to understand how pain works and to give it permission to move out of you. Without your "desire to heal," pain will stay frozen and continue to create illness, death and disease. This is pain's job. Pain was trained by you to signal for attention when attention was needed in specific parts of you. You now ignore the signal so much that this signal has increased itself in order to get your attention. Talk to your pain and ask it to leave your body. Ask your pain to move up and out of you and it will. You will know pain is moving when you begin to feel it move through you. It may begin to rise up in one area quite strongly, and as it drains itself out through the lymphatic system you will feel aches and soreness. This is due to the charge that this energy, that was once a simple signal, has taken on.

In the past I have taught you to kick, hit or scream to release your charge. This keeps you owning your own stuff, and allows you to clear your own stuff without subjecting others (those you relate to) to this charge buried deep in you. With emotional pain, crying is a great release. The longer and bigger the cry – the greater the release within. With mental pain, there may be a big charge from frustration, caused by manipulation or control of you by another. This often causes mental anguish or pain as well as physical pain. When you release such a mental charge, screaming is very helpful. Often, in the original encounter, you wanted to scream in frustration and anger but you didn't. This also applies to cases of terror. Often when you were terrorized, either in this life or another life, you desperately wanted to scream your terror but you didn't. Instead you froze, and fear and terror is stuck in you in this frozen pocket. Screaming will assist you in releasing this charge and allowing the terror-filled emotional pain to rise up and out of you.

With physical body pain, you can best assist your release by talking to your body and reassuring it that you love it. This takes some nurturing skills, and it requires you to not be afraid to touch, rub and hug your own body. Loving it helps you release physical pain. It allows it to know that you do not hate it for making you see or feel your pain. You see, your body has intelligence and, for the most part, you all hate something about your body. Body knows this and is well aware that you do not like it. Just one more enemy that you have created....

But this can all be healed and changed. You can change you. You can change what you carry in you and you can change how your future will now be created. The creator of everything is you... "all of you." How good is your relationship with "all of you?" Do you know "all of you?" Do you care to know "all of you," or are there big areas in you that you know you do not like and you want to stay away from? The days of fragmentation are over, and the days of becoming "one" or "whole" are upon you.

You create everything that happens to you, for you, and around you. Why not look at how parts of you are upset with you for being pushed away? Why not know who you are so you can know what is creating for you? Once you know you, you will not be so upset about accepting all of you. I know because I am the part of you who knows all of you, and I have no problem accepting "all of you." Let go of your rules. Let go of everything you have been taught. Let go of knowing and begin to feel. Begin to intuit.

Begin to feel how you are spirit. Begin to trust that part of you who is totally illogical and totally unafraid. You have trusted the fear for so long. It is now time to "come home to the light of love." It is time to allow love to heal all. Remember, love is acceptance. When you can accept all of you, you will have arrived.

❧

When you begin to become whole you will see how fragmented and separated your life has been. Your life will automatically become fuller as you fill out you. You will stop searching and looking for something to give meaning to your life. You will no longer feel like you don't fit in or like you have something missing. You will become whole and your wholeness will be reflected back to you in many ways. Most of you have always wanted "more." More success, more fame, more children, more money, more attention, more friends, more food, more clothes, more stuff, more of everything. This is a direct reflection of your feeling of lacking part of you.

You do not know what you really want when you rush about to achieve greater success in order to make you more desirable. You are literally making you more desirable to you so that you might accept you. Some of you have given up and you don't want to try to get you to accept you. Others are using stimulants such as caffeine and nicotine and diet pills to make your heart race; and your pulse distracts you from your fear of who you are. Nicotine also numbs you as do your tranquilizers and alcohol and marijuana, so you do not have to feel who you are. You get to numb out so you don't have to deal with you.

You use drugs to the extent that you do because you do not like you. You hate you. The greater your need to numb out, the greater your hatred is. I suggest that you begin to look at this area of you. How do you feel about you? Why do you feel so much anger and self-loathing? How can you begin to love and accept you? How can you begin to know you and gradually build a relationship with all parts of you? How can you begin to end the war you constantly fight with your own body and your own feelings?

You feel like you are the victim of an out-of-control mind and body. You feel like your body fails you and your emotions beat you up (or down), and you feel like your mind criticizes you to death. It is all you. You can learn how to be the creator by knowing that it starts with you and comes back to you. You can begin to work with God and allow God (you) to unwind what you have tangled up. You can allow yourself the flexibility to flow and to open enough to "clear" yourself of what you hold. You hold ill health, and illness, and ill will, and ill thoughts. Let go of ill will and ill harmony.

You will be easier for you to accept if you stop being so stubborn and so set in your ways and habits. You are like a stuck recording and you do not think you are. You think you have it all together and you make excuses and you live in denial. Denial is so strong that you cannot see the forest for the trees. You are stuck in a tree and you think you are free. You are solid as a rock and you think you are fluid. You are fighting to not change, and you will find something "wrong" with anything that tries to force you to change. God forbid, if a little pain should begin to move in you! You will convince yourself that you are wrong or doing something wrong. You will see yourself as unspiritual or off your "blissful" path.

I am now telling you that your path includes letting go of everything that has been blocking you from rising up. This includes physical pain, mental pain and emotional pain. I have saved pain for last because it is your worst enemy. You made it your worst enemy by shutting it up and shoving it as deep in you as you could. Pain is only a signal and now you (as a species in evolution) have turned it into a big, feared monster. You fear pain almost as much as you fear God. God gets the greatest fear charge because God is the cause of most of the pain and suffering according to history. "Why does a loving God allow this to continue?" is a favorite saying on earth. "Why would a loving God allow pain?"

You see, I allow because "I am." You do not know what this means. It means simply that everything "is" and you are part of that great isness. You are me. You allow me and I allow you. You and I are "one." You will not understand this concept for some time yet. But I want you to know that you are allowed total "freedom." That is how much love I have for all parts of myself.

You must learn to "love." You are love and you have forgotten that you are. You pretend to have too much pain and stress to properly love. You will find that as you clear your pain, stress will leave your life. No stress can remain where there is nothing for it to pull on. You are stressed because of the "pull." Pain wants to come out and you pull it back down in you. You do not want your pain to leave because you need it now. You are addicted to pain. You have used pain since the beginning of time and it works for you. You have come to rely more and more on pain, and you have a very big belief in punishment through pain.

Some of you rely on pain so much that you do not realize the extent of abuse around this energy. You often hear a parent say, "My parents took a willow stick to me and it made me strong. It gave me character." Hitting is not good for you. If you wish to use painful techniques, I suggest you become aware of the results of your actions. You are so accustomed to hitting and pushing that you even call it loving. "I did it because I love my child and I don't want to see him grow up out of control." When you think this way you are confused. What you are showing your child is someone who is out of balance in their thinking. You are acting out of a lack of awareness and teaching your children to do the same.

This is, to a large degree, the pattern that has existed on this planet for thousands of years. You are out of balance which makes you out-of-control. Your children grow up learning from parents who don't know how to behave, and so the child never knows how to behave. This cycle continues down through the ages, and now we are going to teach you how to "love you" so that you might teach others from love, rather than from fear. I know that revenge and punishment are very, very popular with you. I know your movies are based on the bad guy getting hurt, and pain has become a golden gift that the good guy is in charge of dispersing. Let's stop dispersing pain on ourselves and on others for a while, shall we? Let's stop wanting to see them "fall." You are creating a "cycle of falling" for you. You are receiving your thoughts because they run through your body.

You are not here to receive and give punishment or revenge. You are here to love and to forgive. Give forgiveness a chance. The act of forgiving is very powerful. When you are feeling forgiveness it runs through your body, not another's body, and so it heals *your* un-forgiveness. You can tell how much you judge you by how much you blame others. You can tell how much you forgive you by how quick you are to forgive others.

Forgiveness is not stupidity. Forgiving is not putting yourself in situations that cause greater pain. Forgiveness is a level of intelligence. When you forgive, you simply "let go" of. You no longer seek justice against another. You no longer sue or strike back. You begin to *know* that you create your reality, and you *know* that you are the one who is evolving. It has nothing to do with the one that you have drawn to learn from. You "let it go" and you get on with your life. You don't hold them to blame for what you create. Now; here is the tricky part; most of you are very into "holding them accountable" for what they do. I highly suggest you stop playing judge and jury in this way. You do not know what you are creating for yourself. You have enough problems in your life without drawing greater drama to you.

As everyone knows "life is just a dream." Lighten up and begin to realize this simple little fact!

❧

Once you begin to see how you are made up of many energies that you do not particularly care for, you will begin to see how easy it is to not like you. These energies are a part of you and they live in you. You will begin to see how this works as you begin to clean you out. Once you touch these energies they will move. They play dead in you and are activated when touched. You can touch them by re-stimulating them through an incident that is similar to what caused them to be held on to in the first place, or you can touch them by your desire to heal. You may even touch them by your desire to know what is in you.

Once you begin to move these energies you will begin to "feel" them. They move you because they are moving in you. You may begin to think that your life is miserable when, in actuality, you are moving the energy that holds misery in you. Once you allow these energies to move, by way of expression, they will feel accepted and no longer be a prisoner inside of you. You are all "feeling" what is in you if you have read this series of books. You have been guided to within and it is impossible to not experience what is within. Some of you are so good at denial that you will suppress even these feelings, but, for the most part, you will move your feelings and you will not like it. How do I know that you will not like it? These feelings would not be trapped in you if you could accept them. Feelings only get trapped and frozen, or crystallized, out of fear.

You see, you create the darkness by taking light and calling it bad, or evil, or awful. Then it stops dead in its tracks and becomes fixed or solid. You then get lumps of energy that block up the flow within you. This is basically how you have become such a sick species, and now it is time to show you how to heal lifetime after lifetime of ill health and ill thinking. You are going to feel better when you drain the darkness out of you. You are going to feel better when pain goes back to its simple little job at being a signal. You are going to feel better when you let go of what "you" are holding on to. You will not like this, and it will not feel good until you have moved enough pain to drain some of your blockages. These pockets of pain have been in you since you were born and have drawn more of the same to you. Some of you even genetically carry the fear and pain of your family. This is not unusual.

As you grow, you begin to know things, and some of the things that you know are things that were decided on by your parents and grandparents in their lives. Cellular memory is in your cells, and your cells came from their cells. When a cell or atom splits, both parts carry the coded intelligence and unintelligence of the whole cell. You are fooling yourself if you think you are any different than those you come from. You may try to avoid them or you may worship them, but the simple fact is that you are them in this particular body. Now; you also carry soul memory from other bodies and other parents and families. This soul has a very, very long memory. You are so much that you do not know. Stop trying to control everything from your end. You have the least awareness of any part of you and you think you have all the answers.

For now, I suggest that you allow yourself to flow with creation, and allow yourself to clean out some of your ancient and not so ancient garbage.

⚜

Once you begin to clear pain, you will actually be a little confused and unsettled. This is due to the fact that pain has been in one place in you for so long, and once it begins to move around you will feel its effects. This is not to say that you won't always like what you feel. Sometimes when pain leaves a certain area it leaves pleasure behind.

This is due to the fact that pleasure and pain are the opposite ends of the same line of energy. If you have had great pain in certain areas of your life, you will feel the pleasure that was buried with the pain. In other words, once you begin to move a pocket of pain, you can be certain that pleasure was shut off and buried with it. It usually takes getting the pain out before you feel the pleasure. Once you feel it, you may continue to run it through you. You do not have to block pain in the future and this, of course, is directly related to blocking pleasure.

Now, for those of you who do not want to touch your pain, or see your pain, you may continue to behave in this manner. It is also possible that you may never touch your pleasure or see your pleasure, as it is the same line of energy. As you learn how energy works, you will no longer "fear" it so. You will begin to see a logical progression of energy, and you will see how a pebble thrown into a pond causes ripples. A wrench stuck in your spokes will effectively cause big problems in the further turning of your wheel. And a big pocket of pain in you will effectively block, or shut down, your pleasure in life. Why do you think that you all scream to be saved? It is not so much about what goes on around you; it "is" about how you perceive and feel about what goes on around you.

You are being guided here. You are being guided to look at what makes you up, because what makes you up creates your reality for you. It is energy and energy has magnetic qualities. You will find that like attracts like, and also opposites will attract. This is energy progressing forward and repeating its pattern. This is what energy does.

There is no big mystery. God is not punishing you. You *all* believe in a punishing God. God is acceptance and allows you to do whatever you want. You allow yourself to not know what you do, so I am allowing you to receive information that will be a gift for those who use it wisely. Do not be confused. God does not ask anyone to be in pain. God does, however, ask you to feel and to know what you are, so you might know how you create the pain that you create. To let go of pain is a very big step in letting go of a very big part of your current creating process. If you wish to create pleasure and let go of pain, I highly suggest that you "let go" of pain and allow pleasure to move.

*A*s you begin to see how you have separated and fragmented into spaces within yourself, you will begin to understand how you can create a reality that sometimes overwhelms you and may even feel awful to you. Once you learn to "release" big portions of you, who are separated within you, you will begin to release the creator who has been trying so unsuccessfully to gain your acceptance. Now that you know you have pockets of pent-up, hostile energy in you, you can begin to ask these pockets of pain to release. Once they have released, you will "feel" them. Then you will more than likely clear some anger that is attached and maybe some fear of whatever this situation, or event that caused you to suppress the incident and make it painful, is. Then you may release sorrow. Sorrow is usually attached to any painful event. The sadness would be in direct proportion to the amount of joy that was lost during the event.

Now; if you were shamed or yelled at in front of others, you will release shame as well. This is easy to spot. Usually shame draws "in." Shame does not want attention or recognition. Shame is belief that you are wrong or awful. Once you touch your shame, you will move it. This may cause greater separation in you if you are not able to forgive yourself. You will know if you harbor ill will towards yourself, or not, by your degree of willingness to forgive others. If you do not easily forgive, you can be sure that you will not easily forgive yourself.

Most often, the degree to which you are split and fragmented is directly related to the degree to which you are capable of denying. If you find it easy to pretend that you don't see something, or that you don't recognize what you see, you are very good at denial. Denial allows you to hide yourself from yourself as well as from others. If you hide parts of you from others, in an attempt to please them and be more like them, you are good at hiding you from you in an attempt to please you and be more like what you can accept. So; your measuring sticks are always there for you. If you easily lie to others in order to manipulate them, you will easily lie to you in order to manipulate yourself.

This is a very strong pattern in most of you. You are all hiding parts of you from others and from yourself. Do not be so sure that you know you... you do not. As you begin to realize the extent of your denial, you will see how you are only a very, very tiny part of you. Your consciousness is but a pinpoint of existence compared to the energy pool, or ocean, that makes up the rest of you. How can you possibly create the reality that you want when "you" are such a tiny fraction of you?

*W*hen you first begin to clear pain it will not feel good to you. As you go along you will begin to separate from your pain and you will feel it as less a part of you. As you release this built up energy in enema you will begin to feel relief, and gradually you will feel much lighter. After pain has left you, you will begin to see how easy life can be. You will no longer hurt all the time so you will no longer be struggling with pain. Oh, you don't literally know that you hurt all the time... but you do. If you didn't hurt you would not be so codependent and dependent on stimulation to make you feel better. Some of you can only "feel-good" if you are high on drugs. Some of you can only "feel good" if you just made a big kill in the stock market. Some of you can only "feel good" if someone admires you, and some of you can only "feel good" if you get a promotion or a new dress or car.

You are so out of touch with your pain that you do not know that you have it. It is in you now. You do not create more pain, because you are so full of pain now that more will not fit in you. You simply create situations in your life that will trigger your pain so you can feel it. Once you get a little bit of it to move you get really upset and yell and scream at God, or at someone else. This has always been your pattern. You do not want to feel your pain and you do not want to own your pain. You accuse others of doing things to hurt you because you do not wish to own what you are. Stop being a victim! Begin to acknowledge your pain and you will begin to come out of the victim role. You are the cause of your pain! You have it in you and it draws 'like' to it. This is not punishment; this is simply energy doing what energy does. Energy attracts energy. It gives off signals that say, "This is what I am." These signals attract more because like attracts or magnetizes to like.

Once you begin to see the benefit in releasing pain, you will no longer be so upset with those who assist you. You will begin to see how you are set up in a certain manner that draws certain conditions to you. This can all change. You are all in a state of flux and you all have the ability to become fluid and flowing.

You will find that pain is your last big hurdle in your search for God. Pain has been used to create a belief in its benefits, while pleasure was turned into something evil and sinful. In order to release your hold on pain, you must allow pleasure to be good. You did not create evil by "feeling" your pleasure. A lot of well-meaning scholars decided you would be better off to not feel pleasure. It frightened those who did not have balance in this area. They began to preach morality and a belief in a God who punishes you if you do not deny or reject your pleasurable feelings. They took you way off track with their teachings, and now it is time to come back into balance.

You are going to learn to feel pleasure and know the pleasure of living in you. You may touch you and caress you in any way that you like. Do not punish you by not allowing you to gently massage your body or treat your body in a loving, sexual way. You are living in you and you have been taught to fear touching you. You have also been taught to fear your thoughts regarding sex and you have been taught to fear your feelings. This is so deep in you that we may need a very big crane to hoist it up out of you. You must stop fearing you. You... "the-mind-set-in-judgment," fear the body, the soul and the emotions. You fear every part of you, and you never questioned your teachings before. Someone said, "God hates this or that, and he will cast you into hell." That was enough for you. Fear through intimidation really works!

Now we are going to let it all go. We are going to change how we see ourselves and how we see God. Then we are going to see how we are God the Creator, in charge of creating our own lives. I gave you free will, and I will not allow free will to be snuffed out.

Once you begin to see how you have been doing harm to yourself by holding your pain in, you will want to let it out. Once you agree to let it out, you will begin to see a shift in how you view life. You have always viewed life as painful, and you are fearful of life. You do not believe that you have a good opportunity to "be." You do not believe in the moment. You are so programmed by the past, and so worried about your future, that you do not live in the moment. Once you begin to clear pain you will begin to realize how fearful you are, and you will let go of your fear as the pain drains out of you. Usually you connect pain to a fear, to embed it in your consciousness. Pain is usually always connected to fear in you. Rarely will you clear fear without bringing up some kind of pain, and rarely will you clear pain without bringing up old fears.

Once you begin to see how this progression of energy works, you will see how this process is actually one of moving old, stuck energy so that you might run new, more evolved "energy-thought" through you. Once you clear out those old blocks and begin to "open" to new ways, you will begin to feel like a new person. You will begin to shine with this new energy, and you will glow a little brighter in your role as a light for God. All of you carry a spark of divine grace from the moment you entered this dark dimension. When you begin to realize how you are being turned-on by your own need to evolve, you will see how this spark will lead you. This spark of grace within you is unafraid. It is pure. It needs only one brief moment to ignite.

Once you ignite your spark, it begins to grow "in" you. As this light "in" you begins to grow, it begins to show you anything that is not grace. Grace is the presence of light. You are in a state of grace when you are in light which is love. As you ignite your light of love, you push anything that has been twisted out of shape to the surface. At one time all was light. Now you twist things into evil and darkness, and you no longer view them as light. This allows you to split and divide. If you are not "all one" you do not have to be God. You do not wish to be God because you began to fear God. Once you see how you fear what is you and you call what you fear evil, you will begin to see this denial game that you play.

You have created a great deal of pain around your need to hide your true identity. You are not you. You are God and you are afraid of God because you created fear of anything you do not understand. So now you have fear of you and you do not even know most parts of you. You stop you from knowing by projecting judgment and fear. If you did not fear you, you would not be hiding here in the material realm. If you did not fear you, you would be "open" to the light, and this place called earth would not exist. It is just a wall you decided to build to take you one step further from your origins.

You are actually God and you are hiding from the truth. You live a lie and so you never get to be friends with God. You all search for God but you do not really want to know that *you are* what you search for. How disappointed you will feel at the thought that what you search for is "you." The greater your disappointment at this thought the greater your disapproval of you. You cannot be disappointed in discovering that *you are* what you so desperately search for unless you are totally out of love with you. The more you love you, the greater your relief will be that you have found you. The less you love you, the greater your disappointment will be at finding you as the target of your long, agonizing search.

So; how will you react when you find God at last? I think you already know. How disappointed will you be? That is up to you. You can begin now by loving you enough to clear out of you the things that block your understanding and awareness. A very big block to enlightenment is pain and all that is attached to pain. Can you release pain without going into your blame and resentment? Probably not. You will learn to clear energy that is attached to other lines of energy without acting it out on others. You will learn how to clear without blaming everyone around you for "your feelings." You will learn to recognize what is in you and not try to project it onto another. This will take time but you are here to evolve up out of this mess, and once you do you will see that it was not so difficult after all.

☙❧

Once you begin to "clear" your pain, you will feel awful at times. I don't want you to worry that you will stay in an awful state. You will not. You will drain the energy and heal a giant wound that is in you. If you can "clear" pain, you will no longer take on guilt. Guilt attracts punishment, and punishment is usually some sort of painful experience, or loss that causes mental pain. If you can just touch your pain long enough to own it you will be in the position to release it.

Pain is directly connected to most of your unhappiness. Without pain (the pain you hold in you) you would have a very pleasurable and pleasure filled life. Do you? Do you have day, after day, after day, that is full to the brim with pleasure? Do you know what pleasure is and how it feels? Pleasure is feeling pleased with life. Pleasure is the ability to enjoy it all. Pleasure is a state of free-flowing "innocence." You have not lived in innocence since you ran yourself out of Eden with your guilt and torment. You are not guilty, you are innocent! You are not a victim of God; you are a victim of judgment. You created judgment because you could not believe pleasure was yours. I am giving you back pleasure and taking away pain. Pain and pleasure must come into balance.

You will find that both pain and pleasure have a place in creation. Pain is a signal that says, "Watch out, there's something going against us in this direction. Either choose a new direction or stop and wait." Pain is not an indictment that says, "Okay, you screwed up and now you'll pay the price." Pain was never meant to be a judge handing out punishment. Pain is only a signal. Do not be afraid to feel the pain you have stored away in you, because with that pain you have stored its opposite which is pleasure. Your pleasure is locked away with your pain, and after you release your pain and bring it to the surface so that you might feel it, you will also begin to feel your pleasure. Pain will more than likely come to the surface first. You may, however, feel days of exuberance before you get to your pain. Some of its energy is actually buried under pleasure.

You see, as pain goes down in your subconscious it takes with it many things. One of these things this energy is connected to is your aliveness. Once you release your pain you will feel "alive." This is also true of releasing in general. It is a way of bringing you away from death. Death is the lack of flow of all energy in you. Once you "block off" and "shut up" and "shut down" enough energy, you effectively "shut down" you, and you then stop breathing and living. The breath of being "alive" goes right out of you. To become "alive," you must "open up" and "un-block" you. You must begin to allow the energy to flow through you. Why do you "stop" and "block" and "shut-off" this energy? Because you are afraid of it. You are afraid of what is living inside of you. Your enemy is living right inside of you. You are afraid to look at it and you are afraid to touch it. You are more afraid of pain than you are of anything else. You will allow almost anything if it promises to not be painful.

So; how do I get you to move what scares you the most? You are all searching for God and you do not want a God who says, "Know thyself." You want a God who says, "Here, I will take your pain from you." I have taken your pain in the past and it teaches you nothing. You simply continue to create new pain. So now I will teach you how to be God and have it within your power to take your pain away. If you do not want to it is okay, it is up to you. If you do want to, you will receive balance and pleasure as your reward. It's up to you. You get to have, or not have, what you want. If you truly desire pleasure you will find it hidden under a pile of energy labeled pain. If you are as brave as I believe you to be, you will not find it too difficult to deal with this part of you.

You have many parts of you that you do not know. Get to know you and own you so you no longer must disown parts of you and, in so doing, continue to split and separate you. Separation must end or you will not live forever. You kill you off by fragmenting you to death. The gap between you and your parts is very, very large in certain cases. I know you can pull together and become "one." Wholeness is your objective, and you may get there by owning and accepting (loving) all parts of you!

As long as you remember to be in touch with who you are, you will know what you are creating. As far as you are concerned you could care less about what is making you tick, so you never get to know how that same energy is creating for you. The creative force is you. You may use techniques to allow you to control your mind and direct your energies, and this will work for a time. It is best to clear your circuits and allow you to balance. Then you will automatically create more balance. The gift is in what you create. How long does it last? How happy are you? Does your happiness last for several months or several years? Do you wish to obtain life-long happiness? How can you achieve what is not in you? Everything that is in you is projected forward and out onto what you call "your life." Your life is not a series of accidents. Your life is made up of you. Your life is "what is in you" projected out for you to see. If you do not see what makes you happy, you can simply change what you see by changing what is in you.

Pain and discomfort are in you big time! Do not ignore them. Do not push them further down by trying to push them away. Get strong enough spiritually that you can invite pain and discomfort to show themselves. These energies do not belong knotted-up in you. They belong in the flow. Once they begin to flow and move, they will unknot and become simply a line of energy. Your blocking them and calling them pain or discomfort has created them.

Did you ever notice how certain issues can severely affect certain individuals, while other individuals don't seem bothered at all by these same issues? You, individually or in groups, decide what is painful and awful. You, individually or in groups, decide what is good or bad; right or wrong. You, individually or in groups, determine how you will perceive any action or inaction. You are so confused by what is right or wrong at this point in evolution, that you honestly believe that you are hurt when you are not. You do not all experience the same level of physical pain anymore than you experience the same level of emotional or mental pain. I can cut one of you, and you may hardly feel it and go around bleeding before you notice your cut or wound. Another of you might feel immediate and drastic pain over the smallest cut. You all carry different levels of pain and so you all experience pain from your level. Some of you believe yourself to be sensitive to pain when, in actuality, you are simply full of pain.

You will find that these writings concerning pain will totally turn you off to further information that I give if you are so disconnected from your pain that you never want to touch it or feel it. This is an area that will not be easy for you. In the beginning of this series, I told you that your two greatest fears on earth are concerning sex and concerning death. Death is not feared for the dying, it is feared for the pain that is believed to accompany dying. It is also feared for the pain of punishment after dying. A vengeful God who demands that you suffer for your wrong choices, and who will see to it that you suffer in hell for eternity, is quite a big fear. The bigger the fear the greater the suffering is. The greater the mental anguish, the greater the discomfort and subsequent pain that is due to follow.

You will find that belief in punishment has led you to believe in punishing; and so you punish you in hopes that you will change your ways before you have to die and face the big bully of a God who threatens to burn you in hell for eternity. And so you suffer... you carry your pain and you suffer. And if I say that you can release your pain by allowing it to surface, so you might re-experience it from your new perspective, you will think I am evil and awful and that I want to harm you. I do not wish you harm. I wish you love. To love you is to love and accept all of you. To accept you is to allow you to feel what you are made of and to stop separating and fighting inside of you. You are the one who is punishing you by carrying a pain magnet in you. Let it come to the surface. You will feel it but you will also transform it. Just by being accepted it will begin to shift into something less dark. It will "lighten" the more you allow it to surface and it will gradually dissipate. You will not take on greater pain, for you will have released your pain magnet.

Now; when you begin to "feel" your pain, you will begin to require loving nurturing. It will be a time for quiet and rest. Your life will be affected and you will slow down. The big problem will be this slow down. You hate to slow down let alone "stop." You will learn how to work with your pain and allow it to clear, and it will know that you are finally releasing it and bringing it forward. This will tell it that you have forgiven it, and it will turn back into energy. Once out of you, it will no longer hold the personality you have projected onto it. It will begin to travel out of your body by way of your system, and you may begin to feel twinges of energy as it goes. If all goes well you will be free of the core of your pain in a few brief months.

For those who have begun to release pain already, I suggest you communicate with it and give it permission to enter your consciousness. To be hidden in the subconscious for so long has made it fearful of you. Once you tell it that it is being set free, you can then begin to work with it as it goes. This is no different than clearing your emotional bodies by crying and "feeling" your emotions. You will now clear your physical body of pain by allowing the pain to come into your consciousness. Will you enjoy this part of your healing? No, you will not. It is similar to being traumatized by being shot with an arrow. You are scared to death, and when the doctor comes he says, "We must push this arrow all the way through you to get it out." Once feeling this was plenty for you, and you will surely not want to do what this doctor is suggesting. You, however, have an arrow stuck in you and you can see how this will complicate your life. So you say, "Yes get it out so I can go on living." Well, you have an arrow stuck deep in you and I am suggesting that it come out. It's up to you. I am only your doctor. You get to make your choices and then you live with them. I wish you well with this big decision.

I know that some of you have experienced, or rather re-experienced, a lot of emotional as well as mental pain. The physical level is the last level to clear. Energy moves from the mental to the emotional and then on to the physical bodies. You will do well with this. You have been well-prepared, and some of you have dealt with a few pains of a physical nature as you have healed your emotional and mental bodies. You are loved and you are being given an opportunity to be your own savior. Take it. The power is within each of you....

As you learn to love you, you will begin to feel okay about your feelings. Most of your feelings are out of reach simply because you do not wish to be in touch with them. Feelings have always been hidden and pushed away. Most of you do not know how to accurately describe your feelings without being confused as to what you are describing. You are not how you feel, but you do believe that you are. If you feel bad, you believe that your day is bad. If your day drags into two days or more of bad feelings, you then conclude that your week is bad. If your week goes on into next week, with more bad feelings, you conclude that your whole month is a bad month. This goes on until you are convinced that entire years are bad. You have even come to the ironic conclusion that you are bad for having these feelings that you so desperately want to rid yourself from. You are not the cause of your bad feelings anymore than they are the cause of your existence. You feel! It is part of what you do in order to exist as a human organism.

You are not your feelings but you do run your feelings through you. You try to shut them down and now we have traffic congestion in you. We have tunnels in you that are clogged and blocked up with energy build-up. We have freeways in you that are overcrowded and have bumper to bumper traffic. You closed down and now you must reopen to allow traffic to flow smoothly. Do not allow only sleek, low to the ground sports cars by. You must allow all traffic to flow down your freeways. Do not block the trucks and buses and larger vehicles. All carry parts of you, and all are headed in a specific direction of evolution. You do not need to block off parts of you.

What if I should tell you that nature has been trying to balance herself for some time now? What if I were to tell you that you are blocking nature from balancing by not wanting to "feel?" You shut off your feelings so you do not have to feel them. You were once a "feeling, sensitive" being. Now you are very unfeeling or, in some cases, overly sensitive. We must bring you back into balance and you can assist. The first thing to do is to be unafraid of your feelings. Do not fear your soft feelings and do not fear your hard feelings. You have split them up for so long, and now you have the opportunity to allow them to mix together and create balance. Feelings that are too hard will benefit by mixing them with your softer feelings. Feelings that are too soft will benefit by mixing them with feelings that are hard.

Now; I fully understand that you have been taught to suppress certain feelings and to only demonstrate other feelings. I am not asking you to go into your killer feelings and kill, nor am I asking you to go into your victim role and be abused. I am asking you to "feel," not to "act out." Once you learn how you can feel and experience feelings without acting them out, you will begin to *know* a very powerful truth. This truth is that you can be in the power position by "allowing" all to move in you. You give permission or you withhold permission. You "allow" or you "hold back." It's all up to you. You are God in this body. You are not the victim of this body no more than you are the victim of life.

You are in charge. You are God in form. You will become more aware of this as you go along. You will release your hold on fear as you attune with what you already are. You are what you identify yourself with but, for now, I wish you to lose your identity.

Once you begin to feel your pain you will want to run from it. You have been programmed for eons to do so. This will be the first time, since the creation of pain in you, that it will be accepted and not pushed further down. The acceptance of pain will have remarkable effects on you. You will be accepting your greatest enemy. There is no one that you despise more than pain. More money is spent on relief from pain and suffering than on anything else in this world.

Once you begin to see the benefits of clearing and releasing pain, you will begin to understand energy and how it works. You may push parts of you away for many lifetimes in an attempt to avoid owning what you are, but in the end, you will want to accept all parts of you in order to evolve to the next level of creation. You are becoming God. You are becoming "awareness." This means you will no longer be unaware, confused and hurt. The owning and acceptance of the part of you who carries your pain will allow you to come full circle and know God. You once knew God and you did not hurt. You now hurt because you forgot God. You are changing this now, and I do not wish you to be upset with you for returning to awareness through this same veil that you left awareness through.

You will find that as you own all parts of you, you actually begin to connect with all parts, in order to transform them back to their original form. You did not start with pain. It is your destination at this point; it was not your beginning. You began in trust and faith, and you got all confused and wound-up by your lack of acceptance of trust and faith. Now you have an opportunity to unwind and to let go of everything that you are "holding in." If you ask pain to come forward you will be asking your greatest enemy to step into the light and be exposed. Once pain has drained out of you, you will feel so much lighter and you will carry new found power. This is the power of being pleased. Pleasure is attached to sex in your world and you have forgotten how pleasure really feels. Pain has been predominant in your world, and pain has all but sucked the life out of you. I do not say this to frighten you further. I say this to show you how one energy can drain another by becoming a parasite.

So; if you wish to see pleasure and to know pleasure on a daily basis, you will begin to ask your pain to come up and out of you. As you feel it you will stay calm, as you will know you called it forward in order to release it. Once you begin to release it you will find it difficult at times, but you will not run more pain through you than what is buried in your cells already. You really have nothing to lose but pain, and if you would like to be "pleased" with yourself and your life and your choices, I highly suggest this draining of pain. You will find pleasure quite enjoyable. It is not so high and exciting as bliss, but it is your first step towards a blissful existence.

Pleasure will seep into all areas of you, and this will draw a pleasurable life full of pleasurable experiences. Pain is your wall that is blocking pleasure. Pain is ready to come forward in many, as it knows it is trapped. Pain will assist you in releasing it, as it has been pushing to get out of you for years. Do not be afraid of this part of you. Fear of you keeps you separated from you. We are trying to bring you together and no longer pull you apart. Do you feel pulled at by life? This could be a reflection of you pulling you apart by rejecting parts of you. I will tell you now that the easiest way to bring you back into you is to release what you hold, so there is room for the Soul, God, You, Light...... "Love."

❧

Once you begin to see how you are made up of all parts of you, you will wish to stop rejecting those parts that frighten you. You are afraid of God and you are afraid of Satan. God is you and Satan is you. Anything that "is" is also you and you are all that "is." You may not recognize this for some time to come. It is, however, important now to learn to accept and to love all of you. The mission of this entire series of books is to get you into you, so that you might accept and love you. Do not stop short of your mark. Do not be afraid of this part of you that you believe to be evil. Allow yourself to grow beyond pain by releasing pain. If you can do this you will be releasing your greatest fear and hence your greatest block to love. Fear stops love from entering just as love stops fear and dissolves it away. If you can move your fear of pain, you can become clear of pain. If you become clear of pain you will no longer create pain in your life. You will begin to create only pleasure and your life will change dramatically.

So; the choice is yours. You may begin to clear pain by asking it to show itself. You may ask for pleasure which will also stir up your pain. In order for pleasure to move, it must also move the pain that is attached to it and holding it down with it. Once you get your pleasure/pain moving, you will be allowed to feel again. You have shut down your ability to feel love out of the need to stop pain. You have shut down your ability to know love out of your need to shut out pain. You live frightened lives out of fear of what sits inside of you. You may now change what is in you, and you may now begin to love yourself and life and the world. Your blocks are big and you will not readily accept this technique for healing and unblocking yourself, but this information is important for your awareness, and so it is being given here as a gift, in hopes that you will evolve into a place where you might receive it as helpful and enlightening.

So; you may now relax. I'm going to change the subject and allow you to un-tense. You will like my new subject. It is all about money. Money for most of you is tied in to fear, and so to get you in prosperity we have to de-power money and allow you to not need it. If you desperately seek money you are out of balance, and you really seek security or a feeling of being safe and comfortable. Once we can get you to become safe and comfortable "within," you will begin to relax enough to allow money to flow to you. Once it is flowing it will freely come and freely go with no blocks in either direction. Once it is easily flowing into and out of your life, you will have created prosperity. It will be enough to make you happy, and you will not feel like you have to hoard it in order to provide future security and safety for yourself or your offspring.

Once you learn the value of being in the flow, you will no longer wish to build blocks. As you learn to feel the flow, you will gradually give up your need to "hold on to." You will begin to feel safe about letting go. Letting go allows you to flow with creation. Creation is evolving and returning to the creator. You are creation and you are the creator. You are evolving and returning to you. You are the beginning and you are the end. There is no other. You are all that "is." No one else is here. You are playing energy games with yourself and, thereby, frightening yourself. You are now going to stop frightening yourself and begin to love yourself. This is law. The only law that exists is love. There is nothing but love. You are "in" love and pretending that it is something outside of yourself. You are in God and pretending that he is something outside of yourself. You are "all." You do not wish to accept that you are "all," and so you only get to be a fragment. You will change. You will "open." You will "love" you!

※

*O*nce you begin to see how you are causing pain by simply holding on to pain, you will realize the benefits of giving up your hold on pain. Your hold on pain is your need to push pain back down whenever it wants to come up, or come forward. You are so full of pain that you cannot help but feel pain in some area of your life. As you "let go," or release your hold on pain, you will allow yourself the freedom to enjoy a pain-free life. You will come into what is known as pain-free existence. Pain-free existence is directly connected to your ability to give up pain. Can you surrender your hold on pain? Can you be free of pain by allowing it to come up out of you?

You must be aware by now that you carry energy and you hoard energy and you block energy. Some of what you hoard is beginning to spoil and become toxic. It is best to allow what is in you to move, and you will not feel good about this. You will not want to move what is in you, because you have spent so many lifetimes trying to hold it still or keep it buried. You are at the point of no return. You have taken on so much awareness that your parts are aware of what you are aware of. They now know what you know. They are alive and they have intellect as well as you do. They are part of you and you are disconnected from them. I suggest you reconnect with your pain, and allow it to move through you in order to get out of you. You do not belong in pain, you belong in pleasure. You have a center and that center is ready to reclaim you. You have been living in extremes for too long. You are stretched out of shape and it is time to reclaim your balance. Balance is in the center. It is good to be centered. You can stand evenly when you are in your center.

As you continue to let go of your pain, you will begin to feel the charge of power drain out of it. You will begin to feel less fearful of pain and also less fearful of other energies that are stored in you. You will feel as though you are becoming the whole of you. You will no longer fear parts of you as you now do. Your biggest enemy that you have unconsciously created in you is pain.

Once you siphon off the built-up pain, you will begin to feel less pressure. This pressure has been held against you by you holding the pain down. Let the pain up, and you release the pressure that has built up behind it, in order to give it momentum to get out. It knows it is to go up, not down. It knows its path has been changed by your fear of it. It knows you are pushing down so it pushes back at you - not out of fear, and not out of revenge or attack. It pushes back because "up" is its natural direction, or course.

It knows it is supposed to go "up" and you keep saying "go down." It is like pushing a diver back down when he knows it is time to come up for air. He will fight for his life to get air because air keeps him alive. He dies without air, and the part of you who is carrying pain will die if you do not allow him to surface. He will exhaust himself and will no longer work for you. Then the physical part of the body where this pain is located will go dead also, and this physical part will shut down. Do you get aches where you didn't use to? It could be pain trying to release. Do you see older people go cripple with age or lose mobility? It could be pain that was never released. Do you see hearts stop working and legs become feeble?

You kill yourselves in many ways and one of these is by suppressing your pain. In the same way that you can heal, by bringing up old hurts in the mental or emotional body to release them, you may also heal by bringing up old hurts in the physical body to release them. This is what I will call retracing. It is an activating of information that is buried at a cellular level, in order to retrigger and discharge the original electrical charge. You can retrace or re-experience a pain, and bring it back "alive" by so doing. To be alive is to end the death in those particular cells. To suppress is to bring an end to. To die. To bring back to life is to recall or recollect. The recollection process is very powerful in assisting you to become all that you are. This Second Coming is your savior coming to save you. You will literally be saving you from you. This process *will* work!

Once you begin to understand how you are connected to all parts of "you," you will begin to see how if you 'shut off' or 'shut in' a part of you, it directly affects you (the rest of you). So; everything that you hide, or push away, or shut down, is going to be affecting not only you but it will also affect your world. Your world is simply a reflection of you, and so you see in your world what is happening inside of you. If you don't like what you see, you may change what is going on within.

When you begin to clear and release certain energies, you will be activating them and bringing them into view. This means that what you are clearing is what you are seeing. If you have been asking to "clear" and to "heal," you will become aware of these areas that you are healing and clearing by looking at what is being created, or "drawn," into your life. This will give you a good measuring stick for where you are and what you are releasing. Mirrors such as the world around you and people around you can be very handy for this purpose.

As you learn how to "see" what you are doing, you will no longer be so afraid of what you are doing. You will begin to drop the victim role and take responsibility for your creations. You will begin to take on your role of co-creator, and you will begin to flow with what is going on instead of fighting it at every turn. It is easy to slip into the role of frightened child who hides, or yells and screams at every little thing that is not understood. You are growing beyond your childhood by re-enacting the thoughts and beliefs and feelings of your childhood. You have stuffed a great deal of information into your childhood years, mostly because you were confused and smaller than those who bossed you around and yelled at you in order to train you. You still have a great deal to uncover and it will not harm you when it comes to the surface.

As you learn to play an active role in your own re-creative process, you will begin to understand how energy works and how energy affects you. You will see how you are vulnerable to certain people, or maybe certain situations, only because of a prior instance with that particular energy. You will also see how you can discharge or dislodge certain blocks or energy deposits, and allow areas in your own body/psyche/soul to re-open and allow pure energy to flow through you once again. It is basically a psychological letting go. It is releasing blocks of mental and emotionally charged energy in order to "clear" out your creative track.

This track is a pathway within you that distorts and disturbs, and often shuts down the flow of creative energy. Why is it important to reopen this blocked track or pathway? Because you want love! You want to become what you are and what you are is pure. To re-open you to pureness we must drain out that which says, "You are not pure." And that which says, "You are not pure" is big and strong in you because your computer programming has always carried this message. It came from your family, from your religion, from your teachers, from your society, from your friends, from your co-workers, from your children, from your siblings and from your lover. It did not come from God or nature.

The only way to reprogram such strong information is to clear it from its source or core belief. These books have been set up in such a manner as to lead you into one way of thinking and out of another. Then I lead you out of your newly adopted way and into yet another way of seeing how you can create or think. Thinking is the process by which you take on a set, or specific, belief. One belief or one way of seeing a thing will get you stuck in one way. There are many ways in and many ways out of your created messes, misfortunes and misjudgments. Do not condemn any "way" or "path" or "thought" or "belief" and you will be free to accept "all that is."

You are learning and you are growing, and you are just one of a multitude. Your way is not wiser, nor is it better, nor is it weaker, nor is it stronger. You are not more spiritual, nor are you more powerful, nor are they. You and they are exactly the same. If you sit on a mountain and learn about you, you are no less or more God than he who sits in the desert and learns about himself. If you sit on a mountain of money you will learn about you, and if you sit in a hovel barren of wealth you will learn about you. To be poor is not 'better than,' nor is to be rich 'better than.' It all just is.

You create this belief that money is good and poverty is bad. This in turn creates a belief that money is bad and poverty is good. You are stuck in a rut and your rut is judgment. Be happy inside and your state of financial success will only be something to wear or not wear, like a purple shirt. If you're in the mood for purple, okay. If not, forget about it. A purple shirt is not the beginning or the end. Don't let a purple shirt create judgment in you against others or against yourself.

Be happy by being pleased with your self. Be pleased by allowing pain to leave you. Your pleasure in who you are is directly related to your pain. When pain is released pleasure will follow. They are connected. You will be pleased with yourself when you allow yourself to feel pleasure. It will not matter if you wear your favorite purple shirt or no shirt. The pleasure will be coming from within and you will never again require anything from outside to make you pleased. You will be pleased and your pleasure is directly connected to joy and then to bliss. There is a progression to energy and you are now progressing up the ladder to heaven, or your bliss!

*A*s you learn to overcome your fear of certain aspects of your own beingness you will begin to accept your beingness. To fear you is to put you against you. It is to pit you against your own self and it causes great stress and confusion in you. You are better off to accept all aspects of your beingness and this will take a big shift of energy. Your energy has always been your enemy. Now you are going to use energy that has long been pushing you down, to turn you around. You are going to use this same energy to push you up into a new level of awareness. This will cause you to seek out parts of you that are being, or have been, pushed down, and you will begin to allow these parts their freedom.

Once you set a part free it is able to come forward or move into your consciousness. After you allow enough parts to move forward into your conscious life, you will become very aware of these parts. You will basically be allowing yourself to see, or feel, or acknowledge these parts for the first time since their suppression began. This will be a time of confusion for you. You will feel like you are losing your identity when, in actuality, you are simply adding more of you to you. You have been content up until now to be a fraction of yourself, and now, to become more of you, will feel like you have lost the old you. You are not losing the old you. You are expanding and growing. You will not stay immature in your development forever. You will begin to accept this new expanded version of yourself, and you will become grateful to all of you for being you. You will begin to see how the old you is still with you, only now the old you has developed and grown into a less frightened you. This, of course, will take awhile to recognize.

The most difficult part of the awakening process is change. You do not like change. However, you have been changing since time began. Your body changes and your system changes and your cells reconstruct and change. You change constantly and yet change is your greatest opposition. You dislike it immensely. You dislike change, and you hate or fear anything that you cannot control.

Change is out of your control only because you are such a small fragment of your total self. Your total self has greater awareness and understanding.

So, give yourself a rest by letting go of your need to control. Turn your tiny self over to your larger more enlightened self. You no longer get to suppress what frightens you. You are only two to five percent of you. Don't you think it's time to join the other ninety-eight to ninety-five percent of you? Do you want to remain outside or cut off from the rest of you? The only thing that keeps you from you is you. You are separating from you by digging your heels in and refusing to move your beliefs. You think you know best. You think your fearful thoughts are intelligent thoughts. You fear being led astray and yet this is exactly what you are doing. You are leading, or rather, pushing you astray. You have traditional beliefs that have kept you grounded and sinking for eons. Let go of your tradition. New times are upon you. Let go of your need to do things your way, or what you have been programmed to believe is the right way.

There is no right way! Give it up! Let go of your thought patterns in order to evolve. I will tell you now that to 'feel you' is what you now require. If you do not believe me it is okay. You are the one who benefits or gains by learning to expand. If you want to stay where you are, then stay. I only tell you a way out of "where you are" because you are all screaming so loudly to be saved. It is impossible to save you and not have you rebel.

You are at a point in your evolution where you will only go so far and then you rebel. Your fear and impatience get control of you, and you freak out and you rebel. You will find that salvation is now yours for the asking. However: since you so strongly believe your way to be the right way you will be allowed to save yourself. Steps will be given, directions will be offered, insights will be shared, and you will get to decide whether or not you are ready to accept what is being offered. You will not be judged, nor will you be criticized for saying "no" to any offer or suggestion given. It has always been a free will universe and it will remain so.

❧

Well, you now seem to think that you can behave in any manner you choose and still get to heaven. Heaven is a state of enlightened awareness, and you get to heaven by choosing to leave hell. Hell is the confusion and darkness of limitation and judgment. When you let go of your desire to hold on to what is causing you confusion you will begin to ascend up out of hell. Confusion is often caused by fear and lack of self-esteem or self-love. You will find that as you grow in self-love you will begin to see yourself as loved, and you will leave your fear behind. You are upset about not being loved, and so you yell and scream at anyone who disagrees with you or is not kind to you.

You see, you are not kind to you, and so you often see others as unkind because you are unkind to you. If you begin to be kind to you in your thoughts, you will draw others who are kind to you. If you know your thoughts, you know how offensive they are towards your own self. If you could tune-in to the arguments that carry on inside of you every day, you would want to scream. Actually, some of you do want to scream but you do not know why. These arguments have become very big and out of control. It is the battle of decision: "Should I just let go and fling all my rage at everyone or should I stay quiet?"

These are angry times and that anger is in you. You do not recognize your anger. You know when you are really upset, but you always find a person or a situation to blame. Your anger is trying to surface and it is directly connected to your pain. If you have a great deal of pain, you will have a great charge of anger attached to it. It is probable that your anger charge is even greater than your pain charge. This is due to the fact that pain accumulates and sucks in more energy by its magnetic pull. You actually are very pissed-off about life in general and you all feel like a victim to something that you call "life." Your favorite funny saying is often "Life Sucks." So why do you think you can all relate to that statement? It is due to your own pain regarding life.

So; when you begin to release your anger, you will eventually get to your pain. After you release your pain you will feel the other side of your anger. Anger is wrapped all-around pain like a big furry cover over a big ball. The ball, or center, is pain, and the fur is everything that the original pain, or magnetic pull, has sucked to it. It draws things that match its field. Pain attracts painful feelings. If pain is in you, it has attracted many other feelings to it. This is a good time to mention that you do not die from clearing and releasing your pain. You do, however, die from keeping your pain. You get to get rid of it by bringing it into your consciousness. You have a great deal of pain if you have a great deal of fear when you read this. It is too painful for you to even begin to think about releasing and, in doing so, feeling your pain. As you learn to build your self-esteem by loving yourself, you will automatically begin to lose your hold or grip on pain. Pain arises when you let go of your need to keep it inside of you. It goes up and into the consciousness once it leaves the subconscious.

Now; when you are dealing with a great deal of pain, I highly suggest that you treat yourself with kindness. Do not get angry at you for clearing pain. Allow you to be in pain until you no longer require pain. Do not judge you one way or another. Begin to know yourself by knowing what is in you. You will begin to know what is in you by knowing your thoughts. Thoughts are very tricky. You catch some and distort some and change some for your benefit. Sometimes you even call thoughts bad when they are not – or good when they are not. Thought created you! You are a thought in evolution, or you are an evolving thought. Continue to evolve. Do not turn in on yourself and collapse. Become a whole, complete thought instead of a fragment of an idea.

You can become whole by coming full circle. You come full circle by knowing yourself, which allows you to stop judging yourself. You are God in action. You are God's imagination in creative flow. Do not stop or block your flowing process. Continue to flow and continue to know that you are "idea." You are creative in nature. You are nature. You are God. God is all. You are all.

❧

You will begin to understand your inner workings and your inner thoughts by bringing them to the surface. You are in such a state of denial and you want to keep it that way. You do not want to bring things up and out of you simply because you judge these things harshly, and that is why you push them down into the vast, unknown corners of you. You will find that you actually have guards who tell you when any part tries to move up out of you. God forbid anything should become known to you by surfacing!

Your whole life seems to revolve around hiding parts of you so everyone will think you are different than what you believe you are. You are so afraid of what you "believe" you are that you develop false behavior patterns, just so no one will get a glimpse of what you "believe" you are. They get to see your mask, and even your mask is not what you "believe" it is. You have become so good at hiding parts of you that you are now frightened of everything that is in you. This is mostly due to the fact that you lost track of what all is "in" you and why you don't want it to come to the surface. So now, the fear of anything coming to the surface has become more frightening or bigger than your fear of what is actually "in" you.

You see; you fear what you are because you hid parts of you out of distaste for them, and now that you are evolving in your thinking, these parts will not appear to be so distasteful to you. You, however, are too afraid to chance facing all of you, so you continue to hide and to suppress things that you could simply face and accept and honor. So; you struggle to keep you separate from you, and now is a time of becoming whole, so you are in for a big tug-of-war within. This will cause stress within and this stress within will cause exhaustion. Do you feel pulled apart and totally exhausted? If you do, something may be on its way "up" to the surface. All parts ascend. All parts go up. You are ascending in ways you do not realize.

This is a very good time to mention self-love. You will go far by loving you enough to accept all parts of you. You will go far by allowing you to rise up and by being intelligent enough to allow "clearing" of your cells. Cells are changing in the body all the time, and it will be good for you to know that yours will no longer send out the same old signals once you have "released" the old message, that tells all your cells that certain parts of you are unacceptable and unlovable. This has caused a great many problems for your physical and mental well-being. Well-being has become not so well and illness has taken over.

Once you let some of your old signals clear out of your cells you will allow new signals in. Hopefully you have learned well and your new signals will be healthy and accepting and encouraging. The old signals say something else and they have brought you down. Now we are going to bring you up. You can go "up" by releasing your hold on what keeps you down. What keeps you down and unable to ascend is your fear. What do you fear more than life and more than dying and more than sex? You fear pain. You do not mind the dying as long as it does not hurt. You do not mind living as long as it does not hurt. Pain is the one big energy you must learn to free yourself from. Once you are free of pain, you will no longer use it to punish yourself or others.

You are at a crossroads. Once you reach your pain you have reached your biggest fear. Once pain is gone, self-punishment will have to change. Self-punishment will no longer exist because pain will no longer work on you. Why? Because you will no longer fear it. If you want to punish a child you take away something they want, not something they fear. The taking away creates a fear of loss. If your child does not fear the loss how can the loss be a punishment? If your child has no fear, or just doesn't care if he loses his television privileges, it is no longer a useful punishment. If you no longer fear pain more than anything else, it is no longer your greatest punishment. Self-punishment is very, very big and you do not realize the extent to which you use it on yourself. You will begin to see, and you will begin to change this pattern once you see how you use it.

Once you can allow yourself to no longer fire parts of you for being inadequate, you will find your appreciation. To appreciate something you must not fire it or dismiss its intention. You must accept things as having value before you can fully appreciate them. Once you devalue parts of yourself you become less than valuable to yourself. Once you become less than valuable, you will feel less than anything that you view as valuable. Once you become less than a thing, you have low self-worth and very little self-esteem. If you want to be valuable and increase your worth in order to raise your "self-worth," you may do so by owning and accepting all parts of you. You do not learn self-love by getting rid of the self or even parts of the self. Every part has a purpose or it would not be in you. God does not cut out parts of himself in order to love all that is God. God is perfection. The only difference between you and God is your level of awareness. You are the part of God who is "becoming" and growing in awareness.

God is constantly "becoming." This is nothing new for God. However, your intelligence has been limited for a reason and this has served a purpose. Now that purpose has been served and it is time to move on to the next step. God is arriving in all his glory "in" you. You are going to become "conscious" or "aware of the fact that you create everything." Can you handle becoming "conscious?" Can you give you what is necessary in order to evolve to the next level? Can you sit still long enough to allow this transformation that is going on inside of you? Will you become so afraid of what is in you that you will separate even further? Will you "get it" and understand that this is not pain being inflicted on you, it is simply a birth taking place? Will you be strong enough to handle what you have created, and be calm enough to look at it without running away from you? You have come to this place by consciously wanting to know the truth and by knowing that God is part of you. Now you can take it to the next step, and begin to "feel" how it is all "you" and how you are all of it.

Once you get yourself headed in the direction of lightness, you will find it very difficult to go back to the heavy darkness. You always get to return if you wish it. It is always an option. Everything is an option and the more you can learn about your ability to create, the greater your ability to create becomes. You will literally begin to "feel" God moving in you as one would feel a small babe in one's womb. Men get to birth this time also. It is no longer the female gift of giving life. This is equal. You each get to see how it feels to know God. The creative force will become very strong in each of you as you allow more and more of your past creative efforts to release and return to the flow. Your direction will change, and instead of sinking from the effort to hold on to all your weighty pain, you will begin to surface and rise above not only the pain, but everything that "is" at your current level of awareness.

You see; pure energy rises up. We are purifying you by teaching you to let go of static energy. A pure energy does not require a body. A pure energy is totally free of any dimensional pull. A pure energy has the electric ability to go anywhere and do anything. Your science has already discovered particles, or subatomic particles, that can move through any mass. This is pure energy. Pure energy is the highest form of energy. There is more than just energy, but you are far too dark and un-evolved to understand, or comprehend, that anything so bizarre could possibly exist. So, for now, we will talk in terms your science can at least relate to.

Once you learn how to become pure energy, you will learn how you created form, or bodies. Bodies are not at all necessary but you did enjoy them in the beginning. Now most of you are quite uncomfortable in your own skin. You are all looking for a way out. This is due to the fact that you held on to things you could have let go of. It's sort of like helping people who are in trouble by giving them a place to stay in your home. Now your home is so full of people who do not really belong there, that you don't know who is you and who is them. You lost track of you by being pushed together with all of them. Now you must keep you and let them go. Only, for you, it feels like letting them go is actually losing part of you. You want to hold on to all parts of you, but they do not belong in you because they were not you in the beginning.

You adopted them, and now there are so many of them in you (or your house) that you are all starving for food and stretching and pushing at the walls of your house. There is a big panic and famine and riot going on right inside of your house from overcrowding. So; what did you decide to do? You began to move out in order to escape!

This became the start of loss of consciousness for the body. Now you are moving back in and this causes the others you once invited to share your house to feel squeezed out; and they are popping to the surface and going back where they came from.

You see; you are going back home to you and they are going back home to themselves. Things that are not part of you will no longer pretend to be; and things that you pretend are part of you, just to fit in, will begin to fall away. Pretense is ending as the veil is lifting, and you are coming back home to the light of love. You will not feel good in the light of love at first. It will feel uncomfortable to you because your comfort zone has been in the dark places in fear. You are coming into the light and it hurts your vision at first. You will adjust and you will learn to love again.

❧

Once you begin to see how you are creating what you will be in your future, you will be grateful to know that you are in the creative flow. To know that you take part in your own creation is to know that you are not a victim of anything or anyone. You get to make you into what you want to be, and you get to realize your goals as spirit. You are not just a body with a will and a mind. You are spirit! You are the part of creation that is the creator, as well as being a creation. You might say that you create it and then you wear it or live in it.

You are being prepared to realize how you can take an active, aware and informed role in your evolution. You may continue to fight evolution or you may surrender to it. I suggest surrender, but you may still be into fighting with everything that frightens you. It's up to you as to how you react and respond to the creative force. You may never get in the flow or you may just "give up" and go with it. Some of you have already stopped fighting in an effort to calm down and have some peace of mind. Others are digging in for one last stand-off, while others do not know how to "give in" to the forces of creation.

You have come a long way and you have changed your vibration just by learning new perspectives. As you learn to work with the part of you who is trying to "clear" your pain and your trauma, you will begin to see how you are but a speck of consciousness compared to spirit. Spirit is in you and spirit has a role to play in your evolution. You may not like or understand spirit's choice, because you are so dense. Once you become less dense you will understand, as you will be at a heightened state of awareness. So; how do we get you to this heightened state of awareness if we do not remove the blocks that keep you down? How does pain come up and out of you if you do not allow it to move? How can you move it out of the body and mind if you will not touch it in order to move it? How do we get pain and trauma out of you without zapping it out? How do we zap it out without injuring you in the process? A good zap of light or current into your pain, and trauma would explode in you and terrify you further.

I know you all want God to simply zap you into perfection but, at this point in your evolution, that is not a viable option. Sure, it's one option but not a smart one. I would lose so many of you to "self-explosion," you would just blow apart or in some cases evaporate. So; I'll try something a little less dramatic and a whole lot more feasible. We'll try to talk you into "allowing" your pain and trauma to move to the surface. Then I will actually ask you to be as still as possible while pain passes through you and leaves your cells to be washed out in enema. You will not like this part of your healing, but it will be the greatest "relief" you have yet known. In certain cases you have been carrying your pain through many lifetimes. It has become a big part of who and what you are. Now that you are changing who and what you are, it was inevitable that your pain would have to go.

I'm sorry but you have to give up pain and self-punishment now. I know that you have used it for eons as a way to discipline your "self" and punish your "self." It is time to let it go. It is time to let it move out of you. If this pain and self-punishment programming stays in you it creates greater pain and punishment. Ask pain to leave and do not be upset when you begin to "feel" it in you. You will be afraid because you have great fear of pain. But your knowledge of what is occurring in you will assist you in this clearing. Your knowledge that you are giving pain a way out of you, will allow you to release a great deal of fear of being a victim to this pain.

Once you have asked pain to move, you will begin to assist it simply by not trying to block its rise. This will allow you to be a participant in the releasing of pain. You will find that most of you will clear your pain in cycles. It will come and go. Then a new layer will come up and go out. Then another layer until it is peeled away. After pain is gone you will experience a very quiet type of knowingness about everything. Your life will begin to quietly change and power will begin to grow in you. This power has always wanted to grow but has been blocked by self-punishment. The very last big clearing you will have to do is pain. After pain everything is easy and your life moves into ease and grace. It takes a while to get down to your core or the center of your pain. You have all been moving in that direction simply because you desire "light." Once you reach the core of your pain, you can lift it up and out of you with little-to-no struggle because you are consciously aware of what you are doing.

Now; since we are dealing with all parts of you, including the physical pain and emotional pain and mental pain, you may require the assistance of certain medications. This is okay. You do not wish to traumatize you further. You will know you are making yourself more comfortable while you release pain. This is not to assist you in numbing out. It is meant to assist you in staying calm through your more painful releases. You are not taking an aspirin to shut down or push down the pain, your "intent" is to allow the pain a path out of you. Your "intent" will keep you from pushing the pain back down into you. This same "intent" will allow the pain to find its way out.

For each of you this will be a little different. Some of you have pain patterns that are stretched through several past lives in many different bodies. These pain patterns are all based in self-punishment. This is a karmic pattern for everyone on earth. Every one of you is into self-punishment, and now that we have "cleared" the judgment part of you, we are ready to clear the prosecutor in you and the sentencing that has been handed down. Your views on right and wrong have a new perception now, and your old law enforcement within your self has begun to change. You are changing and growing in awareness which causes your vibration to speed up. When your vibration speeds up, certain parts of you begin to get shaken right down to their roots. These parts cannot survive in "light." They require a slower vibration in which to survive and multiply. Pain lives in a very slow vibration. If you have begun to move your pain it is due to a speeded up vibration.

The faster you vibrate, the higher you go. Congratulations! You have just graduated to a new level of awareness and it is becoming impossible for pain to live in you. You are fertile. You are no longer moving towards death, you have begun your move towards eternal life!

Once you learn how to use your own body as a healing tool, you will begin to see how everything is not about being a body. The body houses many things and it is past due for a thorough house cleaning. You, on the other hand, do not require so much a house cleaning as you do a memory clean out. You need to remember all that you have so desperately tried to hide from yourself. A great deal of what you hide is in your memory, and you do not wish to access it for fear of it and what it might mean to you now. Simple little things are hidden in you. Maybe you were a child molester in a past life, and you are now a monk or a wonderful father of five children who adore you. You are not going to want to upset yourself by remembering how you may have molested tiny children. You would then be unable to sit in your current position of being the saintly, good father or the self-sacrificing monk.

And what if you were a woman who was married and a mother? You would not wish to know that your son from your last life is now your lover in this life. And how would you feel if you had the greatest love of all in your past life and you were not yet finished with your love affair? You now have children and your daughter begins to date your lover, who died at a very young age in your past life, only you begin to "remember" that he is your lover and was your lover before he was your daughter's boyfriend. How would you feel? Do all of your old romantic feelings come to the surface when you recognize the soul in him? Do you begin to rekindle your lost flame of love? Sometimes you do. Sometimes it is even your child that was your lover, and now the veil is becoming thinner and the denial that is required to play this game of reincarnation in slipping away. You have many confused and frightened souls among you who do not understand their feelings or why they do what they do. You are often "attracted" and you are often "repelled," and you do not have a clue as to why.

You are going to feel a great deal of confusion once you begin to "open up" to the information that is always available to you. You may even feel unsafe from being jarred into consciousness. Once you develop your ability to understand how you are "all things" and so is everyone else, you will not feel so vulnerable to those forces. You will learn that it is okay that you were once an ax murderer or that you killed and maimed as did everyone else. It is a part of the theater! You all pray to be so good and to be righteous, but the bottom line is that you are here to act out a drama. Your dramas change from lifetime to lifetime but it is still an act.

You are acting, as if in a play, and you choose your role before you go out on stage. Some of you even negotiate with other souls to get a better role or a more dramatic role. Some want to be the good guy, some want only to play villains. Some even love getting murdered or killed-off before the show ends. Others want to live so they may be remembered within the context of being a survivor. Still others do not care, because they know that when the curtain comes down you will all come back to life to take your final bows.

It is not important what role you play. It is not important if you are good at what you act at. It is not important how into it you get. It is not even important to do it. You need not give what you do any importance at all.

It is like being in your first production in the first grade. You do not have to be good because you do it for pleasure, or you are producing something for entertainment. You are "creating." Do not judge your creations. They were once great fun for you. You now want to stop this game, or type of entertainment, because it has begun to frighten you. You got so into the play that you think it is real. It is not real. None of it matters.

You can do anything or you can do nothing... it does not matter unless you choose to decide that it does. Is a first grade play that important in the scheme of things? To a first grader it can be life or death, or he could simply care less. You are in the first grade play. If it feels that important to you it is simply your perception. If it doesn't matter much one way or the other, you are closer to the flow. If you get really upset by certain scenes, or acts in the play, you are beginning to feel like it is all that you have or all that you are. It is not. You are a great deal more than this tiny point of focus.

You will, at some point in your clearing, begin to get very upset about life and all that it has done to you. You feel like you are a tiny speck in this universe, and you believe you are being pushed and pulled like a ping-pong ball or a yo-yo on a string. You are not a victim or a ball bouncing off objects. You are the hand that holds the paddle in order to hit the ball and keep it bouncing. You are the creator of the play and of the game. It was a simple diversion. It was like a daydream. You began to fantasize and you got so into your daydream, and all of your possibilities, that you forgot how to come back to consciousness. Now you are being drawn back into consciousness a little at a time, so as not to upset you all at once.

This way you get a little bit of truth a little at a time. Should I give you total truth all at once, you would be so afraid that your anger would come up and push the truth further away. This way we get you a little angry and upset, and you calm down enough to digest what is said. Then, when you are ready for another dose of truth, you get another small dose. You would not forgive me if I destroyed your little fantasy world in one big swipe. You would feel stripped of everything that you believe you are. You would feel so enraged that you would never again (in this lifetime anyway) begin to listen to anything that remotely resembled the truth.

You are only afraid of the truth because it will erase the lie. The lie has been in place to protect the game. The game is to come into this world, or enter this stage, pretending to be limited and in a costume with a script or agenda. There is no agenda. You use this so you will not remember the truth. The truth is that you just left this stage yesterday and you were someone's mother. Today you must come back and act as though you are the sexy lover of that same soul. How can you possibly have sex with someone who was just a child at your breast? Easy! You create the veil of "forgetfulness" and voilà! "All" is forgotten and you can get sexually attracted to the soul who was just your son. Oh, and before that he was your mother and before that he was your father and you were his son. It's all very confusing to you because you get to conveniently forget. To forget is to play the game. Do not judge you for playing the game. You are now moving to a new level of awareness which will allow the way in which you play the game to change.

❧

*A*s I believe so I am. This little phrase sums up your body. You simply are what you believe. If you believe you are good you will be good, and if you believe you are bad you will be bad. You do not require a change of spirit; you simply require a change of mind. So; look at how you have changed your mind since you began to learn how things might be, or how you might not have all the answers. You are learning and growing in awareness. As you approach new levels you may not understand why you "feel" the way you do. You may feel uncomfortable. This is due to the fact that you are breaking out of your old programming and you are leaving old habitual belief systems behind. This will not be your comfort zone.

Your comfort zone is actually to feel what you felt in the nest. When you return to the nest it has strong memory attachments for you. When you meet someone who has your same programming, you will be strongly pulled by their magnetic field. You are attracted to this person. What attracts you is something that makes you feel good about them. This something is what you recognize from your past and it has a comfortable feeling to you. You desire this return to the nest feeling, and yet you are breaking out of old modes of operation so this feeling is also repelling to you. All of a sudden you find yourself confused. What do I want? What don't I want? What is right? What is wrong? What is good? What is bad? All your life you have put everything into these few categories. Now I come to you and say, "Let go of right/wrong, good/bad, you do not need them. They are a lie." This will not take hold in you for some time. Everything that you currently "know" and "believe" will fight this new programming. You will not be able to change such deep belief systems overnight.

So; as you read and hate what you read, please remember that you will change your mind in time. You will not always be stuck in your current position. You will not always be as limited as you now are. You will not always be who you now are. You are changing and you are growing. This is evolution, and "believe in it or not" it will continue to exist and you will continue to be a part of it. You can evolve consciously, or you can go kicking and screaming and holding on to the old beliefs. Either way, evolution is at hand. You may call it doomsday or the end of the world, but it is all the same. It is you becoming aware of the fact that you are God. It is more of a birth and a beginning than it is an ending. It is the point where the plant bursts out of the seed and begins to sprout. It is a glorious time for mankind, and this glory will be "realized" at some point in your evolution. It is not all painful change. It will actually get easy for you, and then it will become a pleasure.

After the pleasure phase will come joy. Life will become a joy to live. You will be filled with spirit and with joy. At first you may fight this new merger, but you will give in and you will progress and you will find love. This is where your peace and comfort are moving. You are moving out of a pain-filled comfort zone and into a peace-filled zone. You cannot have pain and peace together. Pain does not coexist with peace. You must let pain go. Allow it to move to the surface in order to move on, so peace can take up the space vacated in you by pain. Allow pain to leave and this will allow peace to enter.

❧

As you learn to control your own creative ability, you will begin to see how you have created in areas you do not wish to stay in. Once you learn how you create for yourself you can begin to create in new, more inspired directions. You may even begin to create from pleasure instead of from pain. This, of course, is based on the assumption that you have "released" enough pain to become less pain energy and more pleasure energy. You will find that once you have been afraid of pain, you will have a difficult time explaining how you are love. After all, how can one be "love" if one is fear based?

So; as you learn to see your creative energy, you will also learn to see just what is and has been created. If you have always created from pleasure you will know it, for your life will be pleasure-full and joyful without any effort at all. If, on the other hand, you are full of pain you will have created many emotional pains for yourself, as well as physical and mental or imagined pains. This is due to the fact that you are creating from a pain base. How did you get a pain base? You began to see certain situations as very painful. You saw "being abandoned by parents" as awful and painful. You saw "being yelled at" as awful and painful. You saw "being stripped of your clothes while everyone laughed at your nakedness" to be painful. You saw "being talked about" as painful. You saw "being lied to" as painful. You saw "being judged as stupid" or "looked down upon" as painful. You also saw "being looked up to" as painful. It became such a responsibility and a burden to be the one who set the pace and the standards. You saw "being alone" as painful. Some now see "being in the company of others" as painful.

You see; you create your pain and then you hold it inside of you. Big pains and little pains are in you. You create by what you are, and what you are is pain!

❧

Once you begin to create from a base of pleasure, you will begin to realize how you have never been a victim of anything. You have simply been a product of your own inner environment. You have been projecting "what you are inside" towards the outside. You have been pushing what is "in" you towards the outer realms of you. You cannot see what you are not. If it is not "in" you it cannot be projected out in the world for you to see. The place that you call the real world is simply a projection of many inner worlds.

As you learn to release what is in you, you will begin to change what you project. Many of you believe the world to be painful and you, of course, believe this because you are full of pain. As you learn to release your hold on pain, you will begin to "lighten-up." You will begin to free yourself of a very big charge of energy that is in you and is often offensive to you. You will let go of the worst of you and begin to operate from the best of you. Right now you operate from pain and from fear of pain. You do not operate from love and freedom from fear. If you can allow your pain to move, you will see yourself, and your entire world, begin to gradually slide down a steep pinnacle that you have been so gingerly and precariously perched on. You are like a hawk who swoops down on everyone to devour what is necessary for his welfare. You need not sit on a steeple of pain in order to keep yourself distant and safe. You can simply allow your steeple of pain to drain down to a more grounded position.

Once you make contact with your pain, it will no longer be so sharp and pointed. Your pain will begin to dull, and you will begin the gradual slide down off of your pain pinnacle. You will gradually slide to the other side of pain which means you will once again reconnect with pleasure. This will take a certain amount of time, since you have been "in pain" for so long that it is your comfort zone. You feel like you need pain to keep you on your toes and to keep you motivated. You have been using pain as a form of motivation since you first began to stifle pain.

So; as you begin to allow pain movement in you, it will begin to flatten and become dull. You will no longer feel its edge, and this will not feel good to those who believe that they require a certain "edge" for business dealings and relationship dealings. You will begin to feel like you are not only losing your edge, you are losing your sharpness and some of you need to feel "sharp" in order to feel on-top-of situations.

So; losing your pain will not necessarily feel all that good at first. After you slide off your pointed fortress and land gently on the solid line of pleasure, you will no longer feel "on top" of your life, nor will you feel like "top dog," nor will you feel successful in certain areas where you now feel successful. You will not be in control and you will not be aggressive in areas you now are. This is due to the fact that your need to "control;" "take charge;" "be in command;" is all based on keeping and feeding your pain. Pain will leave and you will miss it! This is not to upset you. I give you this information so you will "understand." With understanding comes awareness, and awareness brings enlightenment. Once you have enlightenment you have the wisdom that it brings. Wisdom is being wise, and to be wise is to know all and see all, and not be afraid of anything. You are moving towards your own light, and it frightens you in many ways and for many reasons. Do not be afraid. Be "light!"

Once you begin to see how you are not only flesh and bone, you will also realize how each of you is vulnerable to pain. Pain is not so much a definite as it is a choice. You need never be hurt by painful experience if you do not carry "pain charge." Do you ever see another who does not experience pain as strongly as you do? Do you know someone who had what would be a terrible painful experience for you, only they never thought it was such a bad experience? Do you ever see another who bumps a knee or elbow and says, "No it doesn't hurt, honestly I'm okay. It doesn't hurt?" You, on the other hand, may writhe in pain for several minutes when you hit your knee or elbow. Some of you call this a low threshold for pain, but what it actually is, we will call a low level of tolerance.

When you cannot tolerate pain you are already so full of pain that it has become overwhelming. This is when you know you need to release some of what you carry. When you carry huge amounts of pain charge you become "pain sensitive." This is probably at its highest point since creation began. Pain is so big and overwhelming you, that you have become extremely pain sensitive and you feel hurt by the smallest thing. It is like your childhood fairy tale of "The Princess and the Pea." No matter how many mattresses were piled over the tiny pea, the Princess could not sleep for being uncomfortable with the tiny bulge at the very bottom of a huge stack of mattresses.

You have become overwhelmed by pain and over-sensitive to it. It is not such a big feeling as you have made it. You simply have a very big fear attached to it, and this fear continues to grow and send out signals to the nerves and tissues. These signals are sometimes self induced and have no origin. You often call this type of pain psychosomatic. You have created so much pain out of what was not meant to be pain that now you have become proficient at it. *You are a pro at creating what does not exist!*

Now; as you learn to see how pain is getting *way* blown out of proportion, you will wish to bring it back down to size. How? – you ask. By allowing pain to rise up in order to drain out of you. You must allow this energy to deflate and come back down to size. Once pain is in balance you will feel such a "big giant" change in your life. You will not see this change immediately, but you will see it gradually and it will continue until you are pain free.

One of the greatest changes you will see will be a loss of anger. Your anger will begin to automatically discharge itself once you have communicated with and released your pain. Anger is directly connected to pain and most of you realize this on a conscious level. Most of you become very angry and frustrated when you feel pain. I am asking you to feel your pain and stay calm. You need not get angry and frustrated. If you are releasing your pain in a conscious effort you need not get upset about it. Stay calm and be patient while pain leaves you. Usually pain leaves in layers as does all energy.

So; as you release pain you may do so in cycles. This may be a monthly pattern whereby you get more up-and-out of you at certain times of the month. You may find this cycle of release connected to the full of the moon, as the moon is a strong gravity pull and often assists in such energies being moved. Use your calendar to track your progress. You will notice that pain will come up for several months in a row, and as it gets closer to its core you feel it gaining in strength. Once the core is hit and released you will begin to feel its strength drain away. Then there will be several months of releasing the residue which has a much weaker charge.

Now; I want to make it clear to you that this process of releasing pain is for those who are ready. If you start to clear pain in the form of physical aches and pains after reading this book, it simply means that your spirit or soul believes you are ready. For others this will be a conscious "will" choice. You may feel ready to release your pain, or your desire to do so will bring it to the surface. Once you have drained off enough of your fear, you will be allowed to clear your pain. If you have not cleared fear sufficiently you will keep your pain a while longer. After fear goes, you have enough love built up to supply the support necessary to allow movement of pain. Without the support of love, your pain will stay behind your fear and you cannot get to it. Most of you believe in love, however, you are love starved. Once you have fed yourself a great deal of love you will be powerful enough to release pain.

So, anyone who begins to clear physical pain just from reading this book will be okay. You cannot touch your pain if it is still under your fear. If you have released your fear base, you have allowed your pain to be uncovered and now it is ready to move up and out of you. This is one of the greatest steps you will take in the transformation process. Nothing is more powerful for you as a co-creator than releasing this problem. Co-creation is a process by which you create your reality from "all that you are." If "all that you are" is based in pain, you will create from pain. If "all that you are" is based in love, you will create love. This, I promise, will bring you great, great pleasure.

❧

*A*s you begin to see how you are a cellular being with electrical energy running through you, you will begin to realize how you are an energy force. You are charged with your own current. The current that runs through you is part of you, and yet it is mutable and changeable. You may keep your current electrical charges or you may wish to change and create new, more positive charges. Your electrical current is carried through all parts of you, so all parts of you are affected by it. It does you no good to curse your life and your life experiences if you insist on continuing to carry your current energy. If you wish to change your current energy, you may do so by changing your flow. The energy current that is currently "in" you does not do what you want because it is based on a belief in good and evil. If this belief system has been in place in you for more than a dozen lifetimes, it has a pretty good hold on you and you on it.

So; as you begin to let go of your belief in good and evil, you will automatically release some of the charge that holds down your current flow of energy. Once your flow begins to rise, it will upset your current structure "within." You are made up of certain energies and when you begin your transformation process you upset the general balance of these energies. This, of course, is what will eventually bring you out of this far right balance and help you come closer to your center. Once you alleviate some of the electrical charge you will actually set "change" in motion. You will begin to reconstruct your own flow of current and this will change your general makeup. You will literally be changing who and what you are. Your DNA will begin to change once you have selected the correct transformation cycles for yourself.

As you grow into this new you, you will feel uncomfortable and vulnerable. This is primarily due to the fact that you are traveling outside of your comfort zone. Your comfort zone has always been in a very powerful belief in good and evil. Now your comfort zone is switching over to a belief that everything is God. This new zone will take some getting accustomed to. This will allow you to adjust and to realize how your uncomfortable feelings are showing you how you are indeed growing in "light." If you do not feel a change right now, you may be working up to it, depending on where you are in your personal process of evolving. Once you get into big shifting and changing you will know. It will feel very uncomfortable until you have settled into your new zone of belief. Once you settle in, you begin to take root just like you had in your old zone of good and evil belief. This new zone will begin to feel comfortable once your roots have established a strong hook up with your new "everything is God" belief.

So; once you begin to change your direction to settle into a new belief system, your energy flow begins to shift to your new "belief." This new belief is so far away from your old belief that the current of energy does a double path for a while. You actually run energy to the old belief zone (because you need to hold on to what is old and comforting) and to the new belief system at the same time. Your struggle between these two polarities may exhaust you at times. The gradual process of establishing roots in your new belief zone eventually will allow you to stop directing energy into the old belief zone of "good and evil." Once this occurs, anything that is still left in the old belief zone will be pulled to the new belief zone and processed there. This is due to the fact that energy follows thought and the energy flow in the new "everything is God" zone is now taking root and growing stronger than the old belief zone.

So; any old beliefs that were "attached" to the old belief zone now move into the newly established zone.

They obviously will no longer serve a purpose, as the new zone is a totally opposite belief. So they are simply processed right out of the system! You are going to have things come up and out of you, simply because they no longer serve a purpose. Pain does not serve the same purpose once you are embedded in the belief that "everything is God." Pain's old purpose will leave and pain's role will change. You can fight this all you want but it is simply a progression of energy. You may believe you are being punished, but it will still remain a fact that pain leaving you, at this point in your evolution, is simply a progression of energy. You are transforming and growing towards the "light."

I know how you believe this should be a little more magical and mystical and instantaneous, but you are doing a great job from where I stand. You may think you know better, or more about creation and how it should or should not work, but that is based on "should or should not" which does not apply when "everything is God." It served you well when everything was "good or evil," but this is a new age and a new level of awareness, and a whole new world that will soon be manifest "in" you!

꙳

Once you begin to understand how energy works you will realize how you are not a victim. You are simply part of creation and that means that you are part of the flow that is creation. This flow consists of particles of energy. You call it matter, I call it energy. This energy moves and reacts to specific energy influences. You become upset and believe you are being unjustly treated when, in actuality, it is what is "in" you that draws everything to you. You react as though you had nothing to do with anything that you call a bad experience. You do not understand energy and so you sit and feel victimized by an unloving God. Once you learn how to connect the dots and put the big picture together, you will more clearly understand how an energy pattern works.

You do not belong in pain and it is only your buildup of pain that is drawing more pain to you. You do not get punished by God. You attract what you are! You are full of pain, so guess what you will attract? When you let go of pain and come into balance and allow pleasure to take over, what do you think you will attract? This is simple science. Like attracts like and everything has an opposite charge. If you are one thing you have a difficult time attracting the opposite of what you are. You are simply a giant magnetic force!

Now; when you set out to change what you are, you will begin to draw many parts of you to the surface. This, of course, will disturb your normal daily existence and upset your current flow of energy. Your current flow of energy is so up and down that to bring it into a nice even flow will be upsetting to you. You are accustomed to this up and down living and you will feel most uncomfortable in your center. You have been off-balance and out of your center since you came into this body and it does not know balance. Once you find your center you will not be able to hold your position for long. You continue to swing erratically as you are accustomed to this behavior.

You think you are right and you do not know that you are so out of control. How can one who is so erratic be the judge of what is right or wrong? How can anyone who is so out of touch with love possibly judge what love is or how love behaves? How can anyone in an erratic position assume to know what will bring peace and harmony? You must learn to accept and not judge. If you cannot, you will be forced into a position that is very comfortable to you. You will be pulled right back into your old belief of "good and bad" and you will forget about your new belief that "everything is God." Even the mistakes are God. Even what you call evil is God. You say it is evil in an attempt to separate it from you and from God, and so it gets dense. You create the dark by calling it dark.

Two people in love get to be called "light" or good. Two people who hate each other and scream at each other get to be called "dark" or bad. Someone gave you these labels and only for you do they exist. Did I talk about light and dark as though they are separate? Yes, I did! Now I will tell you that I did this as a communication ploy. You can only communicate with me from where you are. If I said, "It is all an illusion, none of it is real so just get over it," I would not be helpful to you. If I communicate to you from where you are in your dream and from what you see, I can help guide you out.

You may get upset about how I change the rules, but it is a way of getting you to retrace and re-step your way out of the illusion you are trapped in. It is all a dream, or an illusion, but to you it looks real, it feels real and the pain is definitely real. I am here to tell you that what you took on, you can unload. If you do not like my advice, that is your choice. I will, however, continue to work through this girl to reach anyone who is willing to come out of the dream, or nightmare, that has been created here. You may follow or you may rebel. It does not matter. You will still be God creating, whether you know it consciously or continue to play the victim of an ogre God on high.

*W*elcome to the universe! This universe is made of energy and light particles. This universe works on a structure based on simple laws or "motions," I will call them. As you move one part it affects all other parts. You are one part and you affect all other parts. As you move you cause the flow to change direction and speed. You block the flow and you redirect the flow simply by your belief and your creative efforts. This flow is "in" you and this universe is "in" you. You are creating a change in the flow by taking in more light and changing your beliefs. This will eventually affect all other parts of you. You will see changes in your body, in your mind and in your life. You will not always like what you see, but this is how you learn to accept. Once you have become accustomed to the fact that you are changing your beliefs, which dramatically affects who you perceive yourself to be, you will understand how you are being "changed" by simply changing your mind! You cannot change your mind and not change you, because you are mind! You are intelligence! You are awareness!

Now; one of the problems you are now having is "awareness." You are consciously feeling the struggle that has always gone on "in" you, only it was in your unconscious self. Now your struggle, and your fear-based self, is being exposed and so you will be subjected to all of your own fears. You will feel a victim, and you will feel the pain that caused this victim role to grow into its current big size and strength. In order to pull you out of this victim role, we have to let you "clear" the charge behind being a victim. This means you will feel your vulnerability and defenselessness. I will warn you now that you will not like feeling defenseless, however, you will find your power in your defenselessness. Once you get over being upset about not being in control, you will begin to see how you are part of a bigger body. You are not your ego identity and you do not have all the answers at this time. The answers are available to you, but your distortion is so great that you can only perceive a tiny bit of reality, or truth, from where you now stand.

Once you begin to understand how you are energy and how energy works, you will no longer buy into this victim role that you currently play. You will see how energy creates and energy repels and energy attracts. Only then will you realize how this is all you being what you are, which is energy. So; don't get upset when you don't like what you see, or feel, or do. You are changing you by changing what you believe, and you will feel everything that is rising up and out of your unconscious old belief system. You are going to feel it because it is in you; not because you are being punished and not because God doesn't love you enough. It will simply rise up out of yourself and you will think, "Oh my God, this feels bad," and you will look for someone or something to blame.

These feelings and this energy have been in you for many lifetimes. Each time you get a new life with a new body, you move in and oh so gradually you begin to unpack your psychological debris that you carry from life to life. In the same way that you carry your patterns from relationship to relationship, you also carry them from lifetime to lifetime. We are breaking the cycle. These patterns will end so that you might find love... your heart light! You have lost heart and this is why 'heart attack' is so big in your society. Don't give up on you now. Once you clear your biggest pain, which is self-hatred and self-loathing, you will have turned the flow of your universe from self-destruction to self-preservation. Preserve you! Take real good care of you! Love you by accepting and allowing your old stuff to come to the surface, in order to allow it a way out of your inner domain. You will do better to unload energy that is blocked and ready to blow. Allow it to leave you, and consciously give it permission to surface and to be on its way.

This is the hard part for you. You have spent your entire life trying not to feel what you are made of; and now I am asking you to release what you are hiding in you, which will cause it to float to the surface and allow you to feel it for the first time, in some cases. Your first reaction will be to go into your natural programming and push anything that doesn't feel good deeper into you. This causes a deeper wound in you, and you will never heal until you allow the wound to heal by allowing the infection to come out. This infection is energy and it can affect all parts of you, which means all parts of your world, or life, as well.

☙❧

Once you begin to understand creation you will automatically begin to understand your creator. You are both creation and creator, and the juice that makes them what they are. You are the whole ball of wax.

Now; I will tell you why you are so pissed off! You are angry at life and at God and at others because you are angry first and foremost at you. You are pissed off and upset about creation and how it works, and yet you are creation and how it works. You are pissed off and upset with God, and yet you are God. You are so confused and uneducated that you believe you are the victim when, in reality, you are the perpetrator. So, basically, you are the good guy and you are the bad guy. You are the evil one and you are the holy one. You are the dead one and you are alive. You are conscious and you are unconscious.

You must begin to see how energy works and how you are energy. Go back to the basics I taught you in Book Ten. Draw a circle. This circle is you. Now draw a line straight through this circle, and at one side of your circle label your line as "Fear." On the other side of your circle label this same line as "Love." Now draw another line making four equal pieces in your circle, similar to cutting a pie in four equal pieces. At one end of this line write "Sorrow" and at the opposite end write "Joy." How can you be sorrow if you are joy? How can you feel pain if you are in health? Pain is connected to elements of the body, or illness of the mind. It is not health and yet it is the opposite of health, which makes it the other end of that line of energy. You will find that all energy runs out from the center – where all energy crosses and merges and becomes "one" or "whole."

The idea here is to become whole so that you are no longer fragmented and scattered. You wanted help! You are receiving help! I can guide you to your center but you are so strongly attached to the outer edges that allow you to stay separate. You love judging and making things and situations right or wrong. Stop it! Let go of your need to judge and you will let go of your need to stay separate from God. Allow you to come in to God by letting go of your hold on judgment. Do not judge anything. Let it all go! Allow it to be. You will not find your center in the extreme edges of you. You will find your center in your heart. Do not judge pain. Do not judge death. Do not judge light. Do not judge dark. It is all you! If you judge anything in you, you will feel it. And since it is "all" in you, I highly suggest you give up judgment. You can do this by practicing forgiveness. Forgive yourself for everything and anything you have ever done or thought about doing. This will allow you to forgive others, for they only reflect to you what you are doing to yourself. Once you have forgiven you, you will no longer require punishment and this will end the illusion of pain.

It's not real folks! None of what you experience in this dream world is real. I am trying to bring you back out of a nightmare, by guiding your thoughts which create your beliefs. If you continue to judge and to deny, you will stay stuck in separation. Even though it is not real it will feel real to you, only because you have gotten so caught up in the drama. Let go of your need for drama by dropping your need for punishment. This can be done by dropping your judgment. Once you drop judgment you actually accept absolutely everything as being okay. You then give everything your stamp of approval, which is good for you because the only thing keeping you in hell is your firm hold on fire, damnation and the judgment that goes with the punishment. If you can let go of judgment and allow everything to be okay, you will not be unfeeling you will be accepting. If you can let go of judgment and allow everything to be okay you will not be apathetic, you will be enlightened enough to drop out of the dream (nightmare).

You will find that your judgment will hold you back from acceptance. The greater your need to hold a judgment, the greater fear you have of your ability as a creator. You will let go of your judgment when you are ready to accept responsibility for your role as creator. Until that time you will continue to require someone or something to blame for everything, be it God or yourself or your neighbor. If you really want to get to heaven you can. Just follow yourself into your heart. Let go of your need to expand and begin to contract, and do not be afraid to contract. It is all in you. Your life evolves around what is in you, and your universe revolves around what is in you. Anything else is only what you are denying. You can call some situation awful, but your condemnation of it does not make it so. You only see through extremes. God is in the center and even he is not separate from you. You are very good at creating big illusions, and now is the time to bust your little game wide open and expose yourself to yourself.

For those of you who do not understand this writing I suggest you go back to Book Seven and reread about the struggle to accept soul.

As you learn to accept all parts of you, you will find it necessary to stop judgment. I know how much you like to judge and put everything into a good or bad category, but it simply is not necessary and it is not whole. To be whole is to accept everything and allow everything. To be whole is to come up out of this three-dimensional belief system. Do you want to? Do you want to go beyond "limited" belief? Do you want to let go of fear and begin to know love? Do you want to rise up above the confusion of restricted beliefs? Do you want to know the God that resides in you?

If you have answered yes to all of these questions, you have the "desire" to rise up to a new level of evolution. This "desire" will create the necessary movement in you and you will begin to "shift" and to "change" within you. As you do so, you will begin to let go of your hold on whatever is keeping you "down" in limited belief. This will then allow whatever has been keeping you "down" in limited believe to surface and release. Since it is surfacing and releasing "in" you, you will feel it! You will not necessarily like it, but you will learn to let go and allow energy to move up and out of you. This, of course, is based on your "desire" to move up and out of limited belief. Your "desire" will create the movement and, if you have great desire, the pain or movement will be great. It has nothing to do with you being punished or you being bad. It simply has to do with a movement of energy "in" you.

You will find that as you feel what is "in" you, you will want to disown it and blame it on someone else. This, of course, explains why you shoved it down "in" you in the first place. You thought you were getting rid of it, but you were actually hiding it so you could ignore it, and eventually go into denial that it is even you. You will find that every feeling, nuance, and accompanying pain has always been "in" you. You just shut off to it, and now, in order to rise above or ascend, you are going to allow it to be seen and heard from again. God is not punishing you! You are "feeling" what has always been "in" you and what you now want to rise up "out" of you. You will allow it to rise, and you may feel that you will never feel good again. You will feel very good once you have let go of these drowning, choking, suffocating feelings. This will allow you to breathe freely and to surface above this dimension. You have been down a long time and now you want to return to the surface. Daylight awaits you and God is there too. You just cannot see God from your blocked and blinded position.

As you learn to stay calm and to "allow" whatever needs to surface, you will begin to feel flooded by the energy. Relax; stay calm; breathe in and out slowly. Allow everything to be okay and it will be. This is only energy leaving and it has been triggered by *your desire* to reach enlightenment. You have a big part of you who is working with you on ascension, and this part knows the end result and the hidden-to-you-now benefits. If you can just remember that this is simply energy leaving you, you will find it easier to not jump into your good guy/bad guy game, which puts you right into your blame/guilt game, which then puts you into judgment and shame. You will be okay! You are just upset because you don't get to be in charge right now. You are being taken out of the driver's seat until you can become conscious while you drive.

You signed on for this. You asked to rise above pain, and the way to rise above pain is to reverse the energy so it goes back out the way it came in. Yes! I know you want it to just be zapped out of you, but you are not in a position to create that yet. Some are, but the numbers are so few that I will direct this information to the vast majority. This is not the quickest way to release pain, but it will work for you because mentally you can handle it. If you were to experience a less drawn out release, you would have mental complications and go into a state of amnesia in order to save your mind. This process is set up in the mind so it might protect you and its own self. This allows the mind to split and fragment in order to save parts of itself. You need to stay whole and conscious for this process of "clearing" to be effective. Therefore you will find this process a little drawn out, but well worth the effort. You need not get upset about your progress. I know how you are into instant gratification, but that will not work for you at this time.

Once you have released enough of your own misery, you will begin to feel less miserable in your life. Then, as misery leaves you, you will begin to feel the joy that has been trapped for so long under the misery. You will no longer have to search for reasons or methods to make you feel good. You will automatically feel good.

Now; as this misery goes, you will actually miss it. Misery has been a very big part of you, and as it leaves with the pain it is attached to, you will feel a great loss. This feeling of loss may turn to sorrow and grief and a feeling of not knowing who you are. This is simply due to the fact that you have always been in pain and misery. Now that you are allowing pain and misery to leave you, you will feel a great loss and a great shift in who you are. Once you go through the initial phase of grieving, or missing this big part of you, you will begin to mellow out and enjoy your new feelings. These new feelings will be connected to peace and acceptance. These feelings have been forming since you began your search for peace and love, or acceptance.

There is always a process in progress whether you feel it or not. Big things happen "in" you whether you know it or not. It is all you creating the new you that you "desire" to be. It's actually a very old you that you once were before you left the God force and went out into your illusion. For eons now, man has tried to define God within limited awareness. Now man is returning to God and will let go of his, or her, need to limit God in any way. You have never in the history of man come close to describing God.

≈◈≈

When you realize how you are part of a giant energy flow, you will begin to see how everything is simply a matter of movement or non-movement. You are moving and flowing in certain areas and you are blocked in others. For the most part you do not wish to let go of your blocks. They have been with you for so long that you want to keep them. You feel like they are a part of you, sort of like a third arm or second head. In the cases that are most predominant, you are actually duplicating certain parts in order to give them more power. You do not require two heads nor do you require a third arm.

As you let go of your need to hold on to your blocks, you will allow these blocks to untangle and unravel and dissolve in an effort to be released into the flow. Once you release them you will miss them. You would miss a second head in the same way that you would miss your first head. So; grief becomes a big part of your inner structure. You lose something and you mourn the loss no matter how little you "consciously" know about this loss. Many of you will go through mild depression and not even realize that you are. This is set up in you as a natural process created to give you time, so you do not go into shock and rejection of the self by suicide. The more you lose internally the greater your grief and depression. Many of you draw an incident into your life that will allow you to grieve openly. You see, it's pretty hard to consciously and openly grieve for something you didn't even know that you had. So; if sorrow gets big in you, you will know that you have "let go" of something big.

As you learn to understand this process of transformation, you will be less and less likely to get upset with others for "your" feelings. You will stop trying to blame everyone else for what you are feeling. You will begin to "allow" your feelings and to validate them, and to really flow with them, even though you may consciously recognize that they are leaving you. As you learn to know the difference between hurt feelings and blocks, you will begin to understand that all hurt feelings are caused by blocks. Blocks are like a giant wound that has accumulated lots of energy and force. This energy constantly draws like a magnet and literally sets up a power base in you. The wound gets bigger and sucks everything into it like a vortex. This is how energy works. The magnetic pull of this wound gets stronger as the energy builds and multiplies. This is when the wound begins to take over your life and affect your relationships and your feelings.

So; what we need to do is release the charge a little at a time, until the wound is less in power. Then we can drain off some of the energy by sending it in a new direction. This, of course, requires a new belief to be installed. As the energy builds around this new belief, it begins to draw more energy to it and it becomes bigger than the wound. This, of course, takes a little time and a lot of "convincing" to keep the new belief in place long enough to start building up energy of its own. Then a curious thing happens. Energy will be sucked out of the old wound, or original hurt feelings, and drawn into the new energy base. It is a matter of power. One is bigger, so its magnetic draw is bigger, so energy gets sucked in that direction. So; if you have fear set in the wound and this fear energy gets sucked over to the new, bigger belief system, the fear will become what it is sucked into. It will become love and acceptance if the bigger power base is love and acceptance.

So; here's the trick. Get a belief system going that is based on what you want to be. Constantly reinforced that belief system in order to get it big, and at some point it will begin to grow and take over. In the same way that fear grew in you and took over, love and acceptance can grow in you and take over. It is a matter of process. It takes a little time, but it works. If you have been reading and learning how to be love and acceptance, you have been creating a new power base in you. When this new power base begins to suck in everything that was in the original wound that created a fear base, you will feel like you are losing big chunks of you and you will feel these chunks of fear. Do not be so upset when you feel your fear. It is being sucked out of you because it no longer has a home in you. Its power base is being sucked dry, and it is confused and flinging itself around in you in order to avoid being sucked into the new belief system of love and acceptance, where it will die and dissolve. On some level you do not want it to die and dissolve. You fear death and you believe it is your second head. It is not. You do not require a second head and so it must go in order for you to balance.

You will lose the pain, as well as the wound, and you will fight it and fear the loss and not want to lose such a big part of you. You will be led gradually and with great patience and love. You will not feel it as love until you have come away with your new belief base in power. However, the greater your pull into the light, the greater your loss of dark. You will not like losing the dark. It has been "you" for a very long time. You will gradually learn to love the light and no longer fear it. You have screamed for love for so long now and I have sent you this information in order to guide you. You will not like love immediately because you are so hooked on fear. This transformation will take time but you have nothing but time. You do not die and you do not end. I am communicating with you, and all that is you is made up of many, many lifetimes. You are not a one life being and you do not end. When you come out of your illusion you will see how you are ongoing and you will no longer require death to frighten yourself further. You will give up death and even, eventually, you will give up birth. You will come and go at will, and you are not so far away from that process as you believe.

I will now end this book. Please stay tuned for further enlightenment and love. Our next book will be titled *The Grace is Ours*. This is a good place to be. You are moving quickly out of your fear base. If you feel a great deal of discomfort you are "moving" a great deal of fear. Love is next. Hold on to love and it will set you free of all fear. You are learning to walk with God, and you are learning to not fear and subsequently hate God. You see, you always hate what you fear. It is a natural progression of energy. So; if you hate God you automatically hate you. This is changing. When fear leaves you, you will be left in "love" with you. Please be patient with you, and do not judge you as you learn to re-create your inner power base. I love and accept you as you are. It is all love; however, we are not through the illusion sufficiently to show you how love works. Next time we will discuss your own ability to create false illusions and discover how the same ability will allow you to create heaven on earth. Go in peace and grace......

God's Pen

I first heard the voice of God in 1988. I was sitting in my back yard reading a book when this big booming voice interrupted with, "I am God and I will not come to you by any other name." I felt like the voice was everywhere – inside of me as well as in the sky around me. I was so frightened that I ran in my bedroom to hide.

This was not the first time that I heard voices. I had been communicating with my own spirit guide or soul for about a year. I guess my depth of fear regarding God, and all that he represented to me at the time, was just too much.

I spent two days trying to avoid the voice of God, which was patiently waiting for me to respond. By the second day I was exhausted from lack of sleep and decided to give in and talk with him. This turned out to be the greatest gift and best decision of my life.

The first book, *God Spoke through Me to Tell You to Speak to Him*, shows my evolution from communicating with my soul to communicating with the Big Guy. It took a couple years for me to be comfortable communicating with God. My fear of a punishing God was big! That has most definitely changed and I now think of God as my partner and best friend.

In the beginning the voice of God would wake me in the middle of the night and tell me it was time to write. He said I had promised to do this work (I assumed he was talking about the soul/spirit me). I would drag myself up to a sitting position and watch in amazement as my hand flew across the page, while I tried to keep up by reading what was being written.

It was always so much fun to wake up the next morning and grab my notebook to see what God had written during the night. After some time the voice stopped waking me and I became comfortable picking up my pen and writing for God first thing in the morning. I think in the beginning I had to be awakened while still semi-conscious from sleep so I wouldn't object too much to the information that was being channeled through me.

As I grew less and less afraid (and more trusting) of God, he was able to communicate greater information. Some of the information is quit controversial, but I felt it important to just let it be and not censor it. I present the writings here to you as they were given to me. I have edited a little (mostly the more personal information regarding myself) and I have used a pen name for privacy reasons. I asked God for a good pen name and he guided me to Liane which (I was told) in Hebrew means "God has answered."

At one point I became a little concerned about my sanity in all this, so I went to a hypnotherapist to find out what I was doing. Under hypnosis I saw this incredibly huge beam of light with a voice coming from within it. It was a giant "loving light" and felt so comforting and kind. It felt like that's where I came from. After that I stopped worrying about my sanity. If this is crazy, I think it's a very good kind of crazy to be….

In loving light, Liane

Loving Light Books

Available at:
Loving Light Books: www.lovinglightbooks.com
Amazon: www.amazon.com
Barnes & Noble: www.barnesandnoble.com

Also Available on Request at Local Bookstores